Wireframing Essentials

An introduction to user experience design

Learn the fundamentals of designing the user experience for applications and websites

Matthew J. Hamm

PUBLISHING

BIRMINGHAM - MUMBAI

Wireframing Essentials
An introduction to user experience design

First published: January 2014

Production Reference: 1200114

Published by Packt Publishing Ltd.
Livery Place
35 Livery Street
Birmingham B3 2PB, UK.

ISBN 978-1-84969-854-2

www.packtpub.com

Cover Image by Aniket Sawant (aniket_sawant_photography@hotmail.com)

Credits

Author
Matthew J. Hamm

Reviewers
Jeromy Condon
Jerome M. Griffith

Acquisition Editors
Andrew Duckworth
Joanne Fitzpatrick

Lead Technical Editor
Sruthi Kutty

Technical Editors
Shiny Poojary
Siddhi Rane
Faisal Siddiqui

Copy Editors
Alisha Aranha
Adithi Shetty

Project Coordinator
Aboli Ambardekar

Proofreader
Paul Hindle

Indexer
Mehreen Deshmukh

Production Coordinator
Nilesh R. Mohite

Cover Work
Nilesh R. Mohite

About the Author

Matthew J. Hamm has been designing visual solutions and interactive user experiences in the Pacific Northwest since the mid 1990s. Specializing in User Experience (UX) design and Information Architecture (IA), Matthew has been active as a full-time in-house designer, UX consultant, freelance designer, and entrepreneur. This has given him a comprehensive view of the many different venues in which websites and applications are designed.

He has worked for and with clients such as Amazon.com, Atlatl Software, Microsoft, SumTotal Systems, Drugstore.com, Napera Networks, Target.com, ToysRus.com, BabiesRus.com, and Imaginarium.com.

When not designing software, he spends his time with his family in Portland, Oregon. In his spare time, he is a linocut printer and gold panning enthusiast. He also enjoys kayaking the beautiful rivers of the Portland area.

I would like to thank my wife, Janelle, for being so supportive at such a busy time in our lives. Though a small number of pages, this book required many late nights and busy weekends to process, write, and illustrate. All of this was added to the hours needed to get a small software startup and running. Many thanks for your patience.

I would also like to thank those who acted as mentors to me early on in my career and who are very much responsible for bringing me into the world of software design: Billy Haffner, Loren Imes, and Troy Turner. Though nearing 20 years since all this started, I am still extremely aware of how you have influenced my life and career, and you have my deepest appreciation.

About the Reviewers

Jeromy Condon is a college instructor and freelance web developer based out of Seattle, Washington. He specializes in custom WordPress theme development and design using HTML5, CSS, PHP, and JavaScript. When he gets a spare moment, he loves to draw, take photographs, and explore the great outdoors.

Professionally, he is a big fan of minimalist, typographic-based design, and mobile user experience study. He teaches web development principles, web graphic design, UX, and web animation at Clover Park Technical College in Tacoma, Washington. He also runs his own freelance web business under the name Rufusmedia, specializing in custom website design and development.

Jerome M. Griffith is a highly motivated graphic designer, web designer/developer, artist, illustrator, and aspiring writer. He has completed many computer graphics, web development, and illustration projects for various clients around USA and in the Republic of Trinidad and Tobago, where he was born and raised. He has more than 17 years of professional experience working with various print, graphic, and web technologies, including food packaging designs, corporate desktop publishing, website design, and website publishing.

While working full-time as a production specialist in a well-known financial establishment in USA, he is also enrolled full-time as an undergraduate student in a distance learning program pursuing a Bachelor of Science degree in Information Technology-Software Emphasis, with projected graduation in 2016. He is building his portfolio and furthering his career in Information Technology with specialization in web development, UI/UX design, software development, and Java Oracle development.

He holds an Associates degree in Visual Communications-Interactive Design (2001) and has earned the industry-recognized CIW JavaScript Specialist, CIW Web Foundations Associate, and CIW Web Design Specialist Certification (2013). He also holds diplomas in Java E-Commerce Application Development and Oracle 9i SQL Development (2005).

Working under the pen name Jerome Matiyas, in his spare time, he writes and illustrates a series of historical fantasy adventure novels entitled the Epic Adventures of Mekonnen (Mekonnen Epic), thus demonstrating skills in original concepts, advanced computer graphics, web design, drawing, and creative writing, with a deep fascination for graphic novels, comic books, animation, movies, cultures, languages, exotic locations, and ancient civilizations.

To view Jerome's portfolio and artwork, go to `Pinevergreenstudios.com` and `mekonnenepic.com`.

www.PacktPub.com

Support files, eBooks, discount offers, and more

You might want to visit www.PacktPub.com for support files and downloads related to your book.

Did you know that Packt offers eBook versions of every book published, with PDF and ePub files available? You can upgrade to the eBook version at www.PacktPub.com and as a print book customer, you are entitled to a discount on the eBook copy. Get in touch with us at service@packtpub.com for more details.

At www.PacktPub.com, you can also read a collection of free technical articles, sign up for a range of free newsletters and receive exclusive discounts and offers on Packt books and eBooks.

http://PacktLib.PacktPub.com

Do you need instant solutions to your IT questions? PacktLib is Packt's online digital book library. Here, you can access, read, and search across Packt's entire library of books.

Why Subscribe?

- Fully searchable across every book published by Packt
- Copy and paste, print, and bookmark content
- On demand and accessible via web browser

Free Access for Packt account holders

If you have an account with Packt at www.PacktPub.com, you can use this to access PacktLib today and view nine entirely free books. Simply use your login credentials for immediate access.

Table of Contents

Preface   **1**

Chapter 1: The Design Process   **5**

A high-level look at the design process   **6**

Research   **7**

The importance of research   8

Designing in an agile environment   10

Information architecture   **10**

Introducing flowchart development   11

Defining the shapes in flowcharts   12

Transitioning to wireframes   15

Usability testing   17

Visual design   **17**

Applying the visual layer   18

Delivery   **19**

Summary   **21**

Chapter 2: Example Project – E-commerce Website   **23**

Research   **24**

Stakeholder interview   25

Competitive analysis   27

Personas   27

Weighing and prioritizing features   29

Information Architecture   **31**

Site map   32

Wireframing pages and content   33

Home page   33

Category pages   38

Product detail page   40

Shopping cart   42

Video library page   43

Mockups	45
Delivery	45
Reviewing the development efforts	**46**
Summary	**46**
Chapter 3: Example Project – Mobile Device Application	**47**
Research	**48**
Stakeholder interview and persona development	48
Weighing features	50
Information Architecture	**51**
Interaction maps	51
Our first map	52
Our refined map	53
Sketches and mockups	55
Creating a new account	55
Finding your team	57
Joining a team	58
Your team's home page	60
Navigation options	61
The Futbol Finder storefront	62
Shopping by product category	65
Usability testing	66
Presenting our deliverables	66
Summary	**67**
Chapter 4: Research Techniques	**69**
Commonly used, effective research techniques	**69**
Stakeholder interviews	70
Design tenet scorecard	70
Competitive analysis	72
Personas and user profiles	73
Creating personas	73
Heuristic evaluation	75
Card sorting	77
Focus groups	77
User surveys	78
Brainstorming	78
Summary	**79**
Chapter 5: Information Architecture and Visual Design Techniques	**81**
Information architecture techniques	**81**
Reality mapping	81
Task flow techniques	84
Page-level detail diagrams	84
Site map diagrams	85

Persona-based task flow diagrams 86
Screenshot interaction maps 86
Paper prototyping 87
Visual design techniques **88**
Mood boards 88
Design scorecard 90
Designing in the browser 91
Summary **92**
Index **93**

Preface

User Experience (UX) design is the act and art of crafting the interface and interactions for a website or application. It is a multidisciplinary career path that requires one to be part visual designer, part social psychologist, a little bit of a developer, and a hint of a project manager, as well as possess a great deal of empathy for those whom you are designing for.

As you will hopefully gather from reading this book, UX design is a career that is responsible for several varied tasks. As with any multidisciplinary career, it is difficult to find anyone with every skill or talent in his or her bag of tricks that are needed. This is to be expected, and I suppose appreciated. It is common to have researchers, scientists, psychologists, developers, and of course, graphic designers change careers to become UX designers to fill the ever-growing need. Each of these bring with them a particular strength that tends to direct them to focus or specialize on a particular aspect of design. Regardless of this unique focus, there are certain universal principles and processes that need to be understood by all.

Whether you are looking to become a professional UX designer or you can't find one and just need to get the job done, the principles and processes discussed in this book will help you get started.

This introduction to user experience design will walk you through what could be described as the industry-standard design process. It will describe the type of research and groundwork that should occur prior to starting your actual design effort. It will also explain several design techniques commonly used by industry professionals. And, it will point out solutions to problems commonly encountered when designing the frontend for websites and applications.

The core philosophy being applied here is as follows:

- User experience design is the act of finding answers to visual and logical questions

- The design process defines the order in which the questions need to be asked
- Design techniques offer a methodology to answer the questions you are asking

On a personal note, I am pleased to offer an introductory summary of my years of experience as a UX designer. I do so with the hope that it will help you avoid the many pitfalls inherent in the software design process. May you find success in all that you design. Let's get started!

What this book covers

Chapter 1, The Design Process, explains the importance of research in the design process.

Chapter 2, Example Project – E-commerce Website, comprises of an example project detailing the process of wireframing a website.

Chapter 3, Example Project – Mobile Device Application, covers how to apply the design process to an example design project for a mobile device.

Chapter 4, Research Techniques, gives a brief description of several more commonly used techniques that we need to familiarize ourselves with.

Chapter 5, Information Architecture and Visual Design Techniques, covers a few of the many Information-Architecture-related techniques that have been developed to assist in the filtering and ordering of information. We will also touch upon some of the visual design techniques that we need to be aware of.

What you need for this book

Having access to a wireframing application will be extremely helpful. This book will not focus on any particular application. Instead, it will cover UX design concepts that can be applied to whichever application you choose to use. Desktop applications such as Axure, Omnigraffle, and Visio are commonly used by design professionals. There are also many web-based wireframing applications that can be used. Some of these include Balsamiq, Moqups, UXPin, HotGloo, and QuirckTools. Many of these online options are free to use or free to try. I would recommend trying several to discover one that best meets your needs.

Who this book is for

This book is an introduction to UX design. If you are interested in learning the basics of the design process, as well as several techniques and methodologies to help you get started designing, then this book is for you.

Conventions

In this book, you will find a number of styles of text that distinguish between different kinds of information. Here are some examples of these styles, and an explanation of their meaning.

Code words in text, database table names, folder names, filenames, file extensions, pathnames, dummy URLs, user input, and Twitter handles are shown as follows: "Imagine that during the research phase of the project with our last client, `futbolfinder.com`."

New terms and **important words** are shown in bold. Words that you see on the screen, in menus or dialog boxes for example, appear in the text like this: "This particular wireframe shows where the user would be taken if they tapped on the **Coach & Referee** category button on the home page."

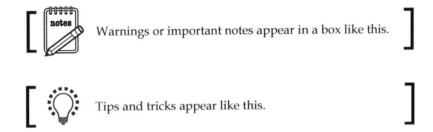

Warnings or important notes appear in a box like this.

Tips and tricks appear like this.

Reader feedback

Feedback from our readers is always welcome. Let us know what you think about this book—what you liked or may have disliked. Reader feedback is important for us to develop titles that you really get the most out of.

To send us general feedback, simply send an e-mail to `feedback@packtpub.com`, and mention the book title through the subject of your message.

If there is a topic that you have expertise in and you are interested in either writing or contributing to a book, see our author guide on `www.packtpub.com/authors`.

Customer support

Now that you are the proud owner of a Packt book, we have a number of things to help you to get the most from your purchase.

Downloading the color images of this book

We also provide you a PDF file that has color images of the screenshots/diagrams used in this book. The color images will help you beter understand the changes in the output. You can download this file from `https://www.packtpub.com/sites/default/files/downloads/8542OT_ColoredImages.pdf`

Errata

Although we have taken every care to ensure the accuracy of our content, mistakes do happen. If you find a mistake in one of our books—maybe a mistake in the text or the code—we would be grateful if you would report this to us. By doing so, you can save other readers from frustration and help us improve subsequent versions of this book. If you find any errata, please report them by visiting `http://www.packtpub.com/submit-errata`, selecting your book, clicking on the **errata submission form** link, and entering the details of your errata. Once your errata are verified, your submission will be accepted and the errata will be uploaded to our website, or added to any list of existing errata, under the Errata section of that title.

Piracy

Piracy of copyright material on the Internet is an ongoing problem across all media. At Packt, we take the protection of our copyright and licenses very seriously. If you come across any illegal copies of our works, in any form, on the Internet, please provide us with the location address or website name immediately so that we can pursue a remedy.

Please contact us at `copyright@packtpub.com` with a link to the suspected pirated material.

We appreciate your help in protecting our authors, and our ability to bring you valuable content.

Questions

You can contact us at `questions@packtpub.com` if you are having a problem with any aspect of the book, and we will do our best to address it.

1
The Design Process

Designing software can be an exhilarating and satisfying experience. But, it can also be a horrifyingly chaotic and frustrating endeavor. There will be many challenges as we work toward simplifying all the complexities of our product. There will be many opinions to consider and compare. Though unfortunate, some of our co-workers may attempt to bully us into accepting their point of view over another. There will also be times when there is a complete lack of opinion. Sometimes no one can see what he or she considers to be the obviously correct solution. And, occasionally, the vision of the product can be so ambiguous that it leaves us without a clue as to what it is we're supposed to be designing.

The best defense against all these situations is a well-defined and evangelized design process. This process will allow us to contain some of the bedlam and confusion that naturally occurs when creating software. The only sure way to succeed is by working together to solve a defined set of problems in a logically directed order.

The first key to employing and maintaining a healthy design process is to possess an understanding of what steps are needed for the project we are working on. We will need to figure out what techniques will help us get the information we are looking for. We will also need to know how to gauge when the time is right to move from one step to the next. It will be important to remain flexible as we assess each new project. To be successful, we will need to tailor the design process for each new product. Documenting and distributing the design process we intend to use will help set expectations. It will also aid our attempt to generate accurate delivery date estimates that project managers and clients will be expecting us to deliver.

This chapter will cover the following topics:

- The importance of research in the design process
- How to map out the structure and task flow of a site or application

- The process of wireframing page-specific content, layout, and navigation required to support tasks a user wishes to complete
- General visual design guidelines about converting wireframes to pixel-perfect mockups
- What software developers will need once designs are complete and ready for development

A high-level look at the design process

The stages of a typical design process and the level of effort generally experienced in each step is illustrated in the following graph. Other designers may break these up a bit differently or may apply different titles to the stages. Regardless of those slight differences, there is a general consensus regarding the common flow and methodology of the UX design process.

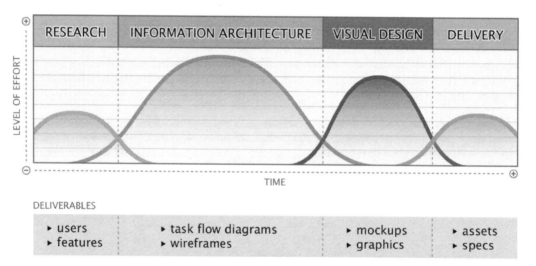

Of course, the actual level of effort will depend on each specific project and the team we are working with. However, this should give us a general idea of the effort required to produce the deliverables listed out after each stage in this chapter.

Let's begin by getting into some of the details and examining each step of the design process. I will explain the goal of each phase, give some helpful tips, bring to your attention some commonly used techniques, and describe how to determine when it's time to move to the next stage in the process.

Research

It may surprise some that the first step of designing is not desig~~n~~ asking questions.

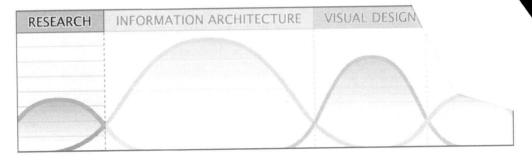

The pressure to start designing as soon as possible is almost always in effect. Mature software designers, developers, and management staff know that research time is a necessary part of the process. In fact, it is the way to kick off the process. However, there are situations when even seasoned professionals forget the importance of this first step. They get caught up in the fervor to get the product out the door and succumb to the pressure of cutting corners by skimping on research that is required to establish a solid informational foundation to start building our software. It is essential to start off by getting answers to several key questions.

These questions are as follows:

- Who is going to use this software or site?
- What tasks does the user wish to accomplish?
- What does the maker of the software or site wish to accomplish? (Not always the same as the preceding question)
- What technology will be used? (Are there any limitations to consider?)
- Why would the public use your software or site over another?
- What is the content needed to support the user in accomplishing their goals?

If we are redesigning an existing site or application, we will likely find it valuable to seek answers to these additional questions:

- What existing features or complexities are hampering or otherwise negatively affecting the user experience?
- What additional features would the user or publisher find helpful in the next version of the product?

the answers to this list of questions may require the application of several
ch techniques. Our research efforts can take the form of competitive analysis to
re our product has the right features or of simply interviewing those who know
o the expected end users will be.

Some of the most commonly used and effective research techniques are mentioned as
follows (see *Chapter 4, Research Techniques* for more details):

- Card sorting
- Focus groups
- User surveys
- Stakeholder interviews
- Design tenets
- Personas and user profiles
- Contextual inquiry
- Heuristic evaluations
- Competitive analysis

The importance of research

The quality and quantity of research we complete will have a significant impact on
how successfully we give the user what they need. It will also influence the amount
of time it takes to complete our designs.

To illustrate how constant an issue this is, I have included the following two
graphics, which I created about 12 or 13 years ago. Though they were aimed at
addressing the issues I was facing with a specific team, it's still relevant and worth
explaining to any team or client you will work with:

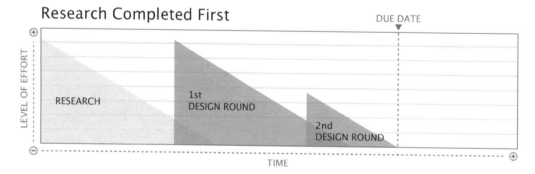

This first chart shows how the process should work. Most, if not all of the research, has been completed up front, that is, before the design work begins. It means a fairly predictable design cycle. The designer knows all of the problems he or she needs to solve. The review of the **1st DESIGN ROUND** usually yields some needed refinements, but not more than that. Time estimates are met, and everyone is happy.

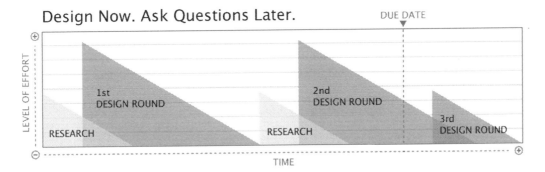

This second graphic shows how things can go wrong and how due dates slip. It's been my experience that some clients or stakeholders just cannot bring themselves to think through all of the requirements and features needed to start a project. We ask them all the necessary questions and they will give some of the details. However, they are just unable to formulate answers to the questions we are asking without seeing our initial round of designs first. Once they see our attempt to wrangle the ambiguity into submission with some sketches or wireframes, they become a veritable fount of information.

When our research attempts yield very little, we are likely to involve the decision maker in the creation of some sketching sessions. So, make these sketches quick, make them messy, but make sure the client is involved in the process. If we attempt to complete a formal round of designs with incomplete information, we are likely to realize that we've just wasted our time.

There is so much that needs to be considered when designing software. When someone is late to introduce new requirements or features in the process, it can feel like the whole thing needs to be thrown out and started over. We can spare ourselves some of the agony by ensuring that the research has been thoroughly pursued and documented. Then, we present the results to the client and team to get their approval and buy in. Ensuring everyone is on the same page from the start will hopefully limit the number of surprises and changes that come in later. And, when they do, it will be with the understanding that these requests are altering the existing expectations. This way, scheduling changes can be discussed as a natural consequence.

Designing in an agile environment

Some designers may find agile development methodologies to be difficult to work with while designing larger comprehensive solutions. Agile is an iterative development methodology that attempts to get a development team to produce faster by reducing the amount of documentation and other overhead, historically gathered before development could begin. It is a reaction to the old **waterfall methodology**, which traditionally had the product mostly or entirely designed and thought out before going into production. This method required a lot of discussion and documentation that slowed production down significantly. Though the waterfall methodology is still in use, it has lost favor due to its slower pace of delivery.

With smaller projects, there shouldn't be too much of a problem getting our research figured out at the start. However, larger and more complex projects can be a challenge. Designing in an agile environment generally requires getting a good head start to get our research and design deliverables completed before the development team needs it. The farther ahead we are, the more time we will have to vet and optimize our work before delivering it to the development team.

To summarize, the quality and quantity of our research will have a direct and relational impact on the quality of the solution we create. Rushing to design a solution without key details, such as who our audience is or what features they might need, will mean a lot of guesswork that may or may not succeed. I always like to think of it as if you want it bad, you get it bad.

Regardless of the methodology we are working with, it is essential that we include research time into our development and design plan.

Information architecture

We transition to the information architecture portion of the design process once we have answered the big questions in the research phase:

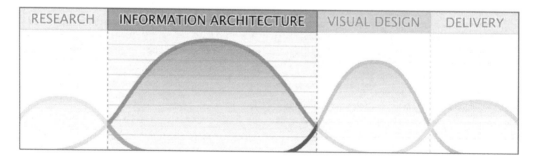

Though I have these steps broken down into distinct stages, it's natural for our research to continue for a while as we begin to change focus. There doesn't necessarily have to be a clean break from one step into the next. Depending on the scope and complexity of the project, we can expect to have different portions of the project in different phases of the design process at any single point in time. The exception to this is the first point in the following list. Our initial research should be aimed at getting enough information to map out a comprehensive diagram of the tasks users wish to accomplish while visiting the site or using the application.

The objectives of this stage are as follows:

1. Create a high-level map of the site or application.
2. Map out the tasks found on each page or screen.
3. Define the content required to support each task.
4. Vet and test our designs.
5. Refine our design solutions.
6. Document the UX patterns.

Introducing flowchart development

This phase is dedicated to the effort of getting the structure of our site or application mapped out. The more complex our project is, the more important it will be to spend the time required to map out the page structure and task flow before we move onto other steps. If we are creating a simple brochure-style website or small application, it lessens the need for a thorough investigation and task flow documentation. Nevertheless, it is a good habit to get into and it helps communicate our plan to the client and/or team. If we are working on a complex website, web app, or other applications, it is absolutely critical that we first map out the task flow and interactions the user will face when attempting to complete a task.

We should consider the creation of a holistic task flow diagram or site map of the product, one of our first primary concerns. If need be, we can shut our office door and produce this map alone based on research we have completed to date. There are situations wherein it is better to shut out the noise of opinion so that we can process everything to come up with a recommended solution. However, I would recommend calling the stakeholders and important team members in for a brainstorming session. I have found it expedites the mapping process immensely when we have everyone in the same room talking over possible solutions.

It can be difficult to give proper credit to the originators of certain commonly used UX techniques. However, we know the **flow process chart** was originally developed by Frank Gilbreth Sr. and presented to the American Society of Mechanical Engineers in 1921 (http://en.wikipedia.org/wiki/Frank_Bunker_Gilbreth,_Sr.).

Mr. Gilbreth has a particularly fascinating history. He worked at refining the physical world as UX designers do in the virtual world. His charting methodology has since been adopted and modified for use in many different industries. The first standardized flowchart methodology specific to UX design was invented by Jesse James Garrett in 2000. More details can be found online at the website of Mr. Garrett (http://jjg.net/ia/visvocab/).

Defining the shapes in flowcharts

If we were to search the Internet for the meaning of flowchart shapes, we would find thousands of examples and possibly a few different interpretations for what each shape and line quality mean. Adopting and applying a deeper visual vernacular can greatly expand the amount of information we can pack into our interaction maps. That being said, we shouldn't consider it a requirement to adopt these charting languages in their entirety. It is good to be familiar with the industry standards for creating flowcharts, and whether we adopt or modify is perfectly acceptable, as long as the flow of information is clearly mapped out and easy to comprehend at a glance. Understanding the basic principles of task flow creation should be enough to get us started.

Here is an example of some of the most common flowchart shapes and their meanings:

Represents the beginning & end of your chart.

A step in the process.

A decision point.

Data manually entered into the computer via a keyboard.

A task requiring manual adjustment by the user.

Represents data being input to or output from the system.

Information shown on the devices display screen.

Flow of the task or process.

Flow option who's availability is conditional.

Here is an example of a simple task flow diagram:

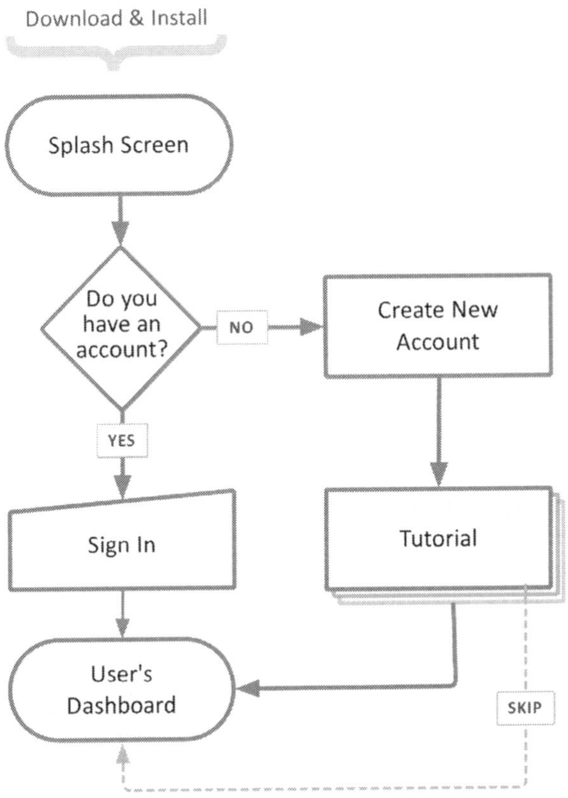

Download & Install

Splash Screen

Do you have an account?

NO

Create New Account

YES

Sign In

Tutorial

User's Dashboard

SKIP

This flowchart example documents the experience expected when installing a piece of software. The primary task here is to determine if the end user has an existing account or if they need to create a new account.

As we can see from the preceding diagram, each rectangle represents a page or task. It starts at the uppermost part of the diagram with **Download & Install** of the application. The reader of the document simply has to follow the arrows to view the options available to the user and the subsequent steps they encounter as they make decisions and enter data.

Here, we can see the experience branch out when the user is asked if they have an existing account. If they do, they are asked to sign in and are taken to their dashboard. If they do not have an existing account, they will be asked to create one. They are then taken to a tutorial to learn how to use the application. It appears that the tutorial consists of multiple pages, and the user will be given a chance to skip and go directly to their dashboard. By using a dashed line, the chart appears to hint that skipping the tutorial is not the preferred path they wish the user to take, but it is available.

Though just a small snippet of a larger experience, we can begin to see how much information can be conveyed at a glance. This is particularly significant when it comes to the branching of decisions. The more options we offer, the more complicated our map becomes. The experience starts to complicate exponentially if each answer to a question leads to more questions. Add a few of these branching questions in a sequence and our experience would be extremely difficult to convey with a text-based explanation.

Let's examine the mundane experience of entering a home in the following flowchart:

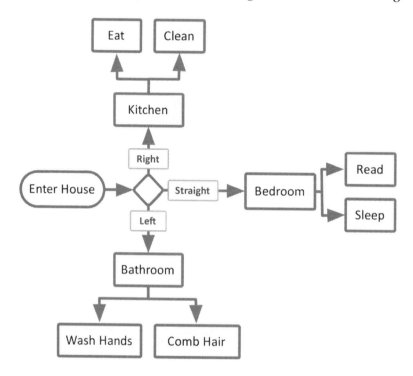

We start by entering the house. Once in, we immediately have many choices to make. They all hinge on which direction we choose to move in. Once we have made our decision, we have another set of unique choices awaiting us. Take a moment to think about how we would describe the same experience using only text. Certainly, it can be done, but it would take far more time and mental processing for the reader to understand. The preceding figure offers a visual solution that can be understood at a glance.

I recently received a functional specification document from a co-worker who was managing a project that my design team was expected to work on. He explained, in moderate detail, how the product would function using only text. Though not a particularly long document, it took us half a day to read through it in an attempt to understand the process he was describing. In the end, none of us had fully grasped the process he was attempting to express. We ended up giving up on the experience and decided to meet with him to talk it through. After some discussion with him to get a clear picture of the task flow he intended, we charted out the same experience on a single page. We cut out about 80 percent of the text, and ended up with an easily understandable document weighing in at a fraction of the size it initially was.

Transitioning to wireframes

Once the project stakeholders have seen our task flow diagram and agree that it is the model they wish to proceed with, it is time to move on to the wireframe stage.

A wireframe is the basic blueprint that illustrates the core form and function found on a single screen of your web page or application. The fidelity of these wireframes will increase in detail as we refine them. However, our first version is likely to just utilize basic black and white outlines and shapes to hint at where navigational elements, text, and graphics will be placed on the screen. The collection of these wireframes should give a comprehensive skeletal view of our entire product.

Here's an example of a first draft wireframe of a website home page:

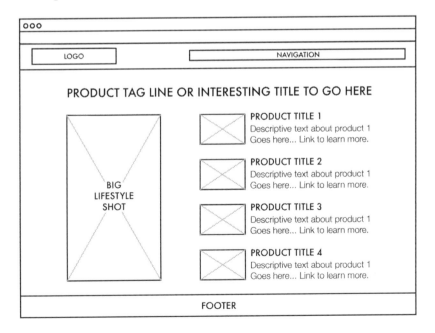

As we can see by examining the preceding wireframe, the content of the page supports one primary task: to direct the user to find the product they would like to learn more about.

To support this task, we have created what we will call "access points" to the different products, shown here as images, headers, and links. However, we don't know what the text will say, what the navigation bar will contain, or what the graphics will look like. All of this requires more discussion and exploration, so we will just block out a space for it and move on.

This process can be much easier if we are redesigning an existing site or application because much of the content can usually be reused. However, if this is the first version of our product, we should not bother ourselves with too much detail to start with. Just imagine the type of content that will be required to support the tasks that need to appear on the page.

As we start to iterate progressive versions of these wireframes by defining and entering page content, the fidelity and detail of our wireframes will increase. As the wireframes progress, we will begin to see where we need to request or create content. We will also need to define and include the optimal navigation model and content taxonomies in our wireframe refinements.

Now would be the time to meet with the development team to explain the current project plan details and any special technical considerations or unusual features. At this point, we will need to figure out if we plan on having our site optimize it's layout for the specific device it is being viewed upon (desktop, tablet, phone, or other mobile devices). This is known as **responsive design**. It has become the standard method for creating websites. It means we are likely to define how our page content and layout will shift to display for each screen type.

The example website I have included in the following chapter is designed with the traditional desktop computer in mind. However, the rise of mobile device usage has many focusing their design efforts on a "mobile first" methodology. This means they start by creating a design optimized for a mobile device and then expand their designs for desktop optimization second. This method will only become more relevant as mobile device usage increases. Regardless of your choice of which to pursue first, you are likely to consider responsive design when designing your wireframes.

There has been much written on the topic of responsive design and a similar technique called **adaptive design** in the past few years. There are many online walkthroughs and video tutorials on the subject that can help you better understand the topic. A search for "responsive design techniques" should get you started on learning more.

Usability testing

Though often saved till after mockups have been generated, now is the time to start testing the usability of our designs. Whether we decide to test our efforts with paper prototypes (see *Chapter 5, Information Architecture and Visual Design Techniques* for more details) or something a bit more formal, it's important to vet our ideas while there is enough time to change them. If we wait to test our designs until after they have been fully fleshed out in mockup form or fully developed, there is often very little we can do to change core functionality.

Some commonly used, effective wireframing techniques are mentioned here (see *Chapter 5, Information Architecture and Visual Design Techniques* for more details):

- Reality mapping
- Site map diagrams
- Persona-based task flow diagrams
- Screenshot interaction maps
- Paper prototypes

Visual design

Once we have everyone agreeing with the design of the task flow, navigation, and general page layout, we will transition to the visual design portion of the design process:

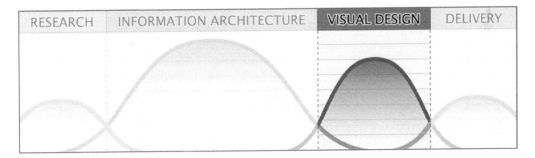

Depending on how you have decided to get to this point, now is generally the time to transition out of your wireframing application (Axure, Omnigraffle, Visio, or others) and open up Photoshop to create your mockups.

The mockups created at this point should be an attempt to portray a **pixel-perfect** representation of the final product. All content and graphics should be defined and put in place. I should note here that the concept of pixel-perfect is beginning to change with the adoption of responsive design and increased website interactivity. When websites were a bit more static and less interactive, it was far easier to create mockups that translated perfectly from Photoshop to a website. Though this is still something to strive for, it should be understood that animations, transitions, and interactive features will create a moving target that will be increasingly more difficult to capture in any design application that produces static images.

Applying the visual layer

As mentioned before, UX design is a multidisciplinary career. Some companies find it easier to divide the design process by hiring information architects who get the details in place. They then pass their files over to graphic designers who *skin* the designs by designing the visual layer.

When the same designer applies the wireframes and visual design, it can be easier to refine the wireframes to a higher level of fidelity. When our wireframes start to take on some of the final mockup qualities, the transition to the visual design phase can be much easier. The generation of mockups is then just a natural extension of what has already been defined. However, if the work is to be divided, I would recommend leaving some room for the graphic designer to explore visual solutions that stray a bit from the wireframes. A good way to do this is to flag the items whose placement or properties should not be altered and let the graphic designer have full sway over the rest.

Content changes at this stage are common. Text and graphics will be explored and updated as the mockups are refined. However, I would offer a word of advice regarding additional features and functionality changes that come in during the visual design phase. It can be very difficult to step back to the wireframe stage once we have started producing mockups. It's tempting to continue making our pixel-perfect designs and roll these changes in at the same time. This can be done, and might be the wisest thing to do if the changes are minor. However, once we start making significant changes to the information architecture, it would be faster and easier to pause our mockup efforts and examine these changes in another set of wireframes. The reason is mostly the speed of execution. The graphic design phase is all about dialing in the visual details, which can take significant effort and time. To examine the feature changes at the same time can slow the process down significantly.

Delivery

The delivery phase of the design process can take place once we have our content developed and mockups approved by the project stakeholders:

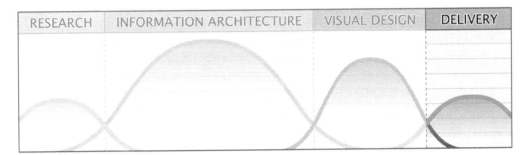

This stage basically breaks down into three tasks:

- Optimizing the graphics for use on the website or application
- Creating specification documents that help the developers build what we have designed
- Reviewing the development work completed to verify that it matches the designs

This last step is by far the most difficult of the three. There is likely to be some significant visual differences between the designs and what has been developed. Even when we have supplied specification documents calling out the margins, kerning, leading, and other attributes, things will be slightly different. The fact of the matter is that the level of control you have over such things in Photoshop is far greater than you have in a web browser. HTML5 and CSS3 have been offered a great deal more control, but often still fall short of what you need.

This issue has actually led to a new career path in the software industry called a **UX developer**. It is for that rare person who has both the ability to code the frontend as well as an eye for design. If we find that our team has significant issues with the translation of mockups to the final design, we may consider hiring someone to help in this capacity.

With this being a rather common problem, we might expect all eyes to be on the end result. We could argue that it is everyone's responsibility to ensure that the product developed matches the mockups as close as possible. After all, there were many eyes on the designs as they were produced. Many opinions were expressed during their creation, and a final agreement made on content, navigation, and it's overall look and feel. Yet, it more often than not falls on the designer to oversee the efforts of the development team's attempt to recreate what is represented in the mockups. At this point, many people hold strong opinions about the details and nuance of the product; however, these seem to fade from the minds of those who held them once the product enters the development phase.

The trick to resolving some of this before it starts is to include the developers earlier on in the design process. It tends to be natural for a wall to build up between the development and design teams. They speak entirely different languages after all, and get called in at different stages of the software development process. It will be of great benefit to all those concerned if we include them early and often.

Furthermore, we will want to ensure they are involved in the earliest discussions so they can weigh in on the technology or technologies that should be used. A discussion about the desired features and our initial ideas about how we think we will attempt to create the user experience should give them enough information to decide which technology to use. Their decision should give us a better idea from the start as to what limitations we may have as well as what options we might have at our disposal.

Beyond this, we should include the development team in subsequent design reviews. This will help them understand why certain decisions were made and point out the significance of certain parts of the interface that should not be altered. Assigning a primary point of contact from the development team who is included in the brainstorming sessions and designer reviews can help our teams stay on the same page without disrupting the entire development team's schedule.

All of this can help prevent the more serious issue of designs and features being significantly altered or cut without notice. The common excuse is, "I know you are very busy" and "I didn't want to bother you." Set the expectation from the start with the entire team that you would like to be involved with any changes that are made to the function, flow, look and feel, and so on. You may have been documenting the product decisions until this point, but there were many eyes on the work, and approval is given by all. If there is a change in what had been approved, it will need to be discussed with the stakeholders.

Summary

Though each new project will require slight variations on the level of effort expended on each of these phases, this design process is for the most part universal. You should expect to follow this process with every project you take on.

Begin researching with the intent to define the users who are going to use the product. Ask the questions required to understand the goals of both the end user and the software creator. Brainstorm to define features that let them complete their desired tasks in an efficient, intuitive, and creative manner.

Once we have those answers, we will start to iterate the information architecture of these features. Begin the process by mapping out the overarching task flow that users will follow through the site or application to complete their objectives. Next, we will define the page-level content and layout required to support the user's efforts in completing their tasks on each page or screen. Then, we test our design solutions to ensure they are intuitive and usable.

With our vision of the overall task flow of the product and page contents documented and vetted, it is time for us to apply the visual design. We will need to create the necessary graphics, fonts, photos, and other visual elements that will replace all of our wireframed elements. Once complete, the designs and their associated graphics and photos will need to be handed off to the development team for production.

Following this process will help dispel ambiguity and will replace it with information and order. It will remove the guesswork and will offer a clear direction in which to take our product.

Now that we have a general understanding of the design process, let's see it in action. The next chapter will walk us through a sample project building an e-commerce website.

2
Example Project – E-commerce Website

Now that we have a general understanding of the design process we should follow, let's put it into action. I have invented a fairly typical client who is in need of some UX design support. He has financial backing and a good head for business, but does not have a lot of experience working with designers. In this chapter, we will work with this client to design an e-commerce website that will entail:

- Educating the client on the design process
- Taking the client through the research phase to define the expected users, features, and product goals
- Creating a map of the entire website to show how the pages are accessed and connected
- Creating and refining wireframes to show how the content, product details, and purchase process are defined

Our client is looking to start a website that sells soccer equipment and other related accessories online. He has put together a small company to make this happen. He has hired someone to develop the backend of his store, purchased the URL www.futbolfinder.com, and has had a logo created. That is the extent of the work that has been completed to date. He knows he needs design support, but cannot justify bringing a full-time designer on, so he has hired us on contract to help design his website.

He has been successful with many other ventures, but this is his first time building an online store. Because of this, we might expect to not only design the website, but also offer guidance on the web-based marketing strategy they might employ. Since his experience working with designers is limited, it will be crucial to meet the client to discuss the design process before any other design work occurs. This will set expectations and get the client thinking about the questions that need to be asked and answered before a realistic solution can be found.

Something to consider

Every project requires a slightly modified design process. For this reason, we won't go through all of the options available in this example. Please refer to the list of design techniques in *Chapter 4, Research Techniques,* and *Chapter 5, Information Architecture and Visual Design Techniques,* for a more detailed suggestion of some of the design techniques our design process might include.

Research

We will need to start this project by gathering information from the client about what the project's purpose is and who is expected to use it. There are many ways to get this information; the most obvious will be speaking directly to the client and any other key decision makers at the company.

Stakeholder interview

The first step is to interview our client (the primary stakeholder).

We will not only need to discuss what type of assistance he is looking for, but take this opportunity to educate him on the design process we expect to use. This will likely bring to light tasks and needs he may not have thought of.

During our first meeting with the client, he tells us he wants to jump right into exploring what the website will look like, but doesn't know exactly where to start. At this point, we walk him through the design process that we expect to follow. We explain that before we can start mocking up the store, a little bit of research will need to be done.

 Something to consider: Now is the time to set all expectations for our involvement with this project. Set limits and document the agreements clearly. Failure to do this now will likely cause frustration at later stages of the design process.

Most of the design deliverables will require multiple revisions before they match the client's expectations. However, if we don't set limitations on how many revision cycles we are comfortable going through, the client can just keep requesting changes. They will insist that the designs aren't exactly ready, and we will get frustrated because of the time it is taking. Furthermore, if we are getting paid in a lump sum rather than by the hour, we will lose money with every revision. We should explain this to the client and document the number of revisions agreed upon for each step in the process. It is appropriate for us to offer more at an additional cost. This will help keep the client's expectations in check, and will help them focus and prioritize their requests.

There are potentially hundreds of questions to answer. At this stage, however, we are interested in finding answers to the following basic questions:

- Who is your target audience?
- How do you tailor the user experience for your target audience?
- What are the features that will entice them to shop at your store over others?
- What features will help you retain customers?

 Something to consider: The design process we are following simply lays out what type of information or level of detail we should be seeking at a particular point in the project. It does not explain how to get that information. For this, we rely on various design techniques. These are exercises or methodologies that help us ask the appropriate questions, and then analyze the answers we receive.

I will illustrate the use of a few of these techniques in the example projects we will walk through. However, it would be impractical to include them all. Because of this, I have listed out many of the commonly used techniques in *Chapter 4, Research Techniques*, and *Chapter 5, Information Architecture and Visual Design Techniques* of this book for you to review and familiarize yourself with. There has been much written about these methodologies that is worth researching further. An experienced UX designer should be familiar with most of these techniques, and should know when it is appropriate to employ them.

Competitive analysis

In addition to our interview, we will examine similar products that are available in the marketplace. In this case, we comb through similar sporting goods websites and document the features and functionalities they contain. Our objective in obtaining this data is to get a sense of what the current marketplace looks like. If we can define what we have to compete against, then we'll have a better idea of how to offer a better experience to the customers.

Personas

During our research gathering, we discuss with our client the types of customers he anticipates visiting the website. Our goal here is to identify and document those primary customer types so we can better aim the product at them directly. We talk through various user traits, but examining the patterns and similarities allows us to simplify our list into three primary user profiles. They are as follows:

- Adult soccer enthusiast fans
- Parents of child youth league soccer players
- Adult soccer players

To help focus the product features for those who will be using them, we created three fictitious profiles also known as "personas". The details of these personas are made up, but they are typical of the customers our client expects to shop at the website most frequently.

We have defined our personas with the following information:

- Name
- Photo
- A quote that describes their personality
- Age
- Location
- Profession
- A brief description of their family life and motivations
- How web or tech savvy they are
- What their shopping priorities are

To help the team keep these personas in mind as we work, we have created a card for each user profile. These can be printed out and shared with the client so we have a constant reminder of who our target market is.

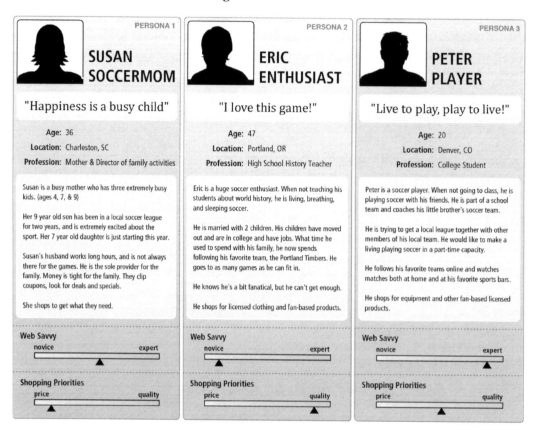

PERSONA 1

SUSAN SOCCERMOM

"Happiness is a busy child"

Age: 36
Location: Charleston, SC
Profession: Mother & Director of family activities

Susan is a busy mother who has three extremely busy kids. (ages 4, 7, & 9)

Her 9 year old son has been in a local soccer league for two years, and is extremely excited about the sport. Her 7 year old daughter is just starting this year.

Susan's husband works long hours, and is not always there for the games. He is the sole provider for the family. Money is tight for the family. They clip coupons, look for deals and specials.

She shops to get what they need.

Web Savvy
novice — expert

Shopping Priorities
price — quality

PERSONA 2

ERIC ENTHUSIAST

"I love this game!"

Age: 47
Location: Portland, OR
Profession: High School History Teacher

Eric is a huge soccer enthusiast. When not teaching his students about world history, he is living, breathing, and sleeping soccer.

He is married with 2 children. His children have moved out and are in college and have jobs. What time he used to spend with his family, he now spends following his favorite team, the Portland Timbers. He goes to as many games as he can fit in.

He knows he's a bit fanatical, but he can't get enough.

He shops for licensed clothing and fan-based products.

Web Savvy
novice — expert

Shopping Priorities
price — quality

PERSONA 3

PETER PLAYER

"Live to play, play to live!"

Age: 20
Location: Denver, CO
Profession: College Student

Peter is a soccer player. When not going to class, he is playing soccer with his friends. He is part of a school team and coaches his little brother's soccer team.

He is trying to get a local league together with other members of his local team. He would like to make a living playing soccer in a part-time capacity.

He follows his favorite teams online and watches matches both at home and at his favorite sports bars.

He shops for equipment and other fan-based licensed products.

Web Savvy
novice — expert

Shopping Priorities
price — quality

Though we could create very detailed personas, we decided that making short ones will be enough in this situation. We have included what we consider the most significant details needed to help give us a general idea of who our primary customers will be.

Something to consider: There has been much documented on the subject of persona creation and usage. I have included some more details on the creation of personas in *Chapter 4, Research Techniques*.

I would also recommend the book *The Persona Lifecycle: Keeping People in Mind Throughout Product Design* by John Pruitt and Tamara Adlin (published by Morgan Kaufmann). It is a particularly thorough examination of the persona creation and implementation process.

Weighing and prioritizing features

The answers we received from our client, competitive analysis, and persona research has helped us create a master list of potential product features. At this point, we attempt to grade and prioritize these features by using a design technique I call the Feature Reality Test.

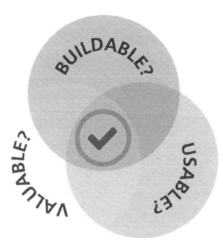

It consists of three criteria that need to be true before any given feature can be included in the project. These criteria are as follows:

- Is it buildable?

    This is really about the technology and resources available. If we were to design this and hand it over to the development staff, could they actually build it with the technology that is available to them? If the answer is yes, the follow-up question to that is how long will it take? It might just require more time and money than it's worth building for. The client will have to weigh the investment required before agreeing to develop the feature.

- Is it usable?

  If we were to create it, would people actually use it? One would think this would be an easy question to answer, but it might require a bit more research to come to a conclusion. This frequently happens with mature websites and software applications. They often cast about for the next big thing, only to choke their user experience with features few will actually use. Certain companies understand the impact and remove these failed features, while others seem to have a more difficult time admitting defeat.

- Is it valuable?

  Sure we can build it, and people will use it, but does it further the goals of either the client or the user? Adding a game to a website might seem of little value, but if it entices customers back to the website, it might be a useful marketing tool. However, if it doesn't offer any return on the investment, it's probably best to cut it from the feature list.

  Using this test, we were able to remove several features that were unrealistic and some that didn't offer significant value to the client or the customer.

With this clearer view of what features are realistic, we have determined that this store should contain the following:

- A home page which will contain lead-in content and access points to the following pages:
    - Product categories
    - List of new products
    - List of sale products
    - List of top-selling products
    - Instructional content
    - About us page
    - Contact us page
    - Link to sign in to an account
    - Links to a social media site

- A page for each product category that contains the following category-specific content:
    - List of subcategories
    - List of new products
    - List of sale products
    - List of top-selling products

- Product detail pages entailing the following:
    - Product image and details
    - Product reviews
    - Product price and shipping
    - Links to related instructional content

- Shopping cart and checkout process:
    - Preview order
    - Access point to check out pages/process

- Instructional content:
    - Content portal
    - Content page

The research we conducted should give us confidence in the decisions made regarding the function and direction of our project. We have defined who our target users are. We have created a list of product features tailored expressly for those users. And, we have scrutinized that list to ensure that they will be valuable, usable, and technically feasible to build. We are now ready to start organizing and developing how these features are accessed and strung together in our website.

Information Architecture

Information Architecture is the act of organizing the data and tasks found in a website or application to ensure that they offer an intuitive and usable set of interfaces to the user. With our list of desired features, pages, and some idea of the content that might be needed, we can move onto defining how everything will fit together.

Site map

We start by creating a site map to examine the pages needed to support the features and tasks we have created during the research phase. This map will help us understand how all these pages connect to each other. Our site map looks like this:

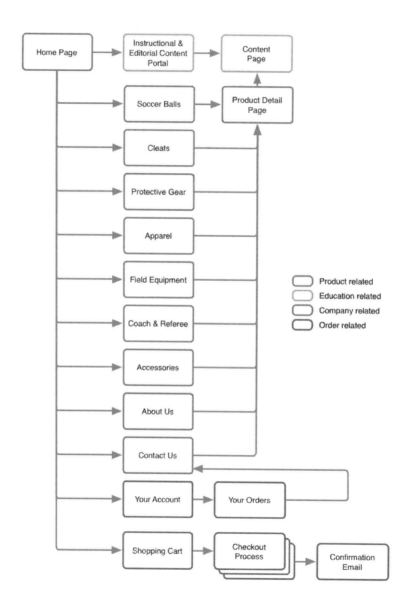

As you can see from this example, our site map is a very simple diagram. Each cell represents a unique web page required to support the features and tasks we expect the user to accomplish while at the site. The arrows connecting the cells show how we expect to get from one page to another. We went a step further and colorized the pages to represent what type of task or content would be found on them. This isn't a required addition, but it may help us understand the different page types better.

Wireframing pages and content

Now that we have the website mapped out and know how the pages connect together, we can start defining the content needed for each page. We will start by working with the client to generate some initial sketches of each page in the site map. These sketches will evolve into more formal wireframes that contain more detail and data with every revision.

 Something to consider: The wireframe process focuses on defining how text, graphics, and other information will be displayed on the page. We attempt to limit our color palette to black and white, and use simple outlines and shapes to represent the placement of this page content. This helps us focus on where the content should reside rather than on how the graphics look or how the text reads. Those are important details to get right, but we will take care of that later.

Home page

We kickoff the wireframing effort with a brainstorming session to examine the content and format of the website's home page. The client has some ideas for the text that is needed to explain and market the products, but does not yet have anything specifically created for it. This is fairly common for new products. We explain that we can get started without it. In fact, the work we do should help define where the text will go and how much of it we will need. Eventually, however, the client will need to make arrangements to have the website content created.

Since we don't have all the details yet, we'll just sketch out a rough outline of where we think text and graphics will be needed to support the tasks and features the client specified earlier. After sketching several possible solutions with the client, we agree on a single layout option. We could agree to wireframing multiple layout options if the client would like to see a few variations cleaned up. However, we can speed up the process significantly if we are able to come to an agreement on a single option during our initial brainstorming session. The sketch of our selected Home page layout looks like this:

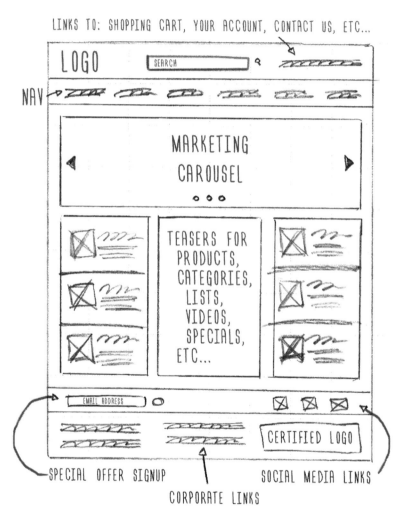

Our sketch is intentionally rough. We try to go through this exercise quickly and keep our sketches loose to keep from getting bogged down by too much detail. We are just attempting to get a fair idea of where everything will go and examine areas that require more thought or investigation.

Our next step will be to clean these sketches up using software specifically created to generate wireframes.

Popular wireframing applications

There are several applications designed specifically to create wireframes. These are available for your desktop computer, and many are available on the Web. Some of the more popular options are:

- Axure (www.axure.com)
- Omnigraffle (www.omnigroup.com/omnigraffle)
- Microsoft Visio (www.office.microsoft.com/en-us/visio)
- Adobe Fireworks (www.adobe.com/products/fireworks.html)
- Balsamiq (www.balsamiq.com/products/mockups)
- MockFlow (www.mockflow.com)
- HotGloo (www.hotgloo.com)
- Mockingbird (www.gomockingbird.com)

There are several others to choose from. Searching for "wireframe applications" should give you these and a few other options to explore.

Initial home page wireframe

As you can see from this new home page wireframe, we were able to add a little bit more detail than we had in our original sketch. We started blocking out where we thought some of the marketing graphics and headlines should go. We placed access points to each of the product categories and defined the general locations where other content would likely reside.

Even with all of these added details, we still have a long list of questions about the page details that need to be answered. Our next objective will be to meet the client to discuss these questions and brainstorm possible solutions. We will continue these meetings until we have enough information to create another round of wireframes.

As we meet the client, he tells us he has decided to hire a writer to create the text needed for the website. We work closely with both the writer and client to ensure they are aware of the amount of text needed, where it should go, and what it should be about. Our designs help drive the direction of this effort. The messaging that is created starts to fill in our wireframes with more detail. Here is how the revised home page wireframe looks:

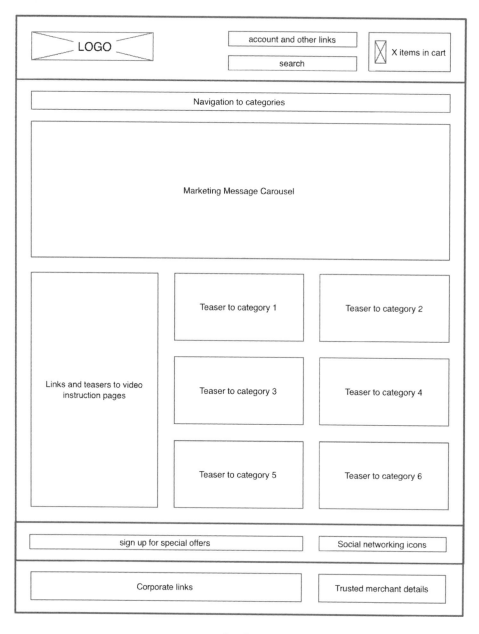

Refined home page wireframe

Upon examination of the following refined home page wireframe, we can see that we were able to make some significant strides with regards to adding detail and content to the page:

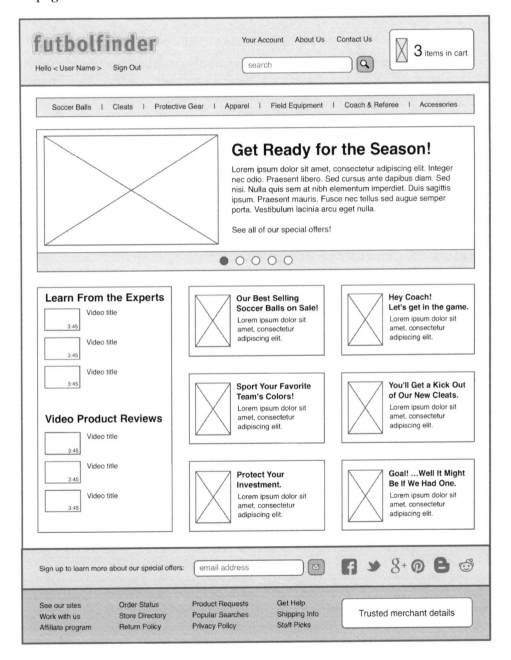

We included a primary method of navigation with the ability to both search and browse the website. We included space for marketing messages, social networking links, the ability to access the video library, and a clear method to access other corporate or company-related information. The client signed off on the page layout and is eagerly waiting for us to move onto the visual design phase.

There is still more text that needs to be generated for the home page. We have placeholder text in several areas that will need to be updated with real text at some point. We can continue refining the wireframes until all the text has been defined or add that in later. The text-based content we receive from the writer may vary from the amount we have placed in our initial page layout. We may need to go back and tweak our designs to accommodate the difference. It would be wise to get this text in place before moving onto the visual design phase for this page.

 Lorem Ipsum is a set of Latin words that are commonly used as placeholder text during the wireframe stage. You can find examples of this online by searching for "Lorem Ipsum" or "Lorem Ipsum Generator."

Lorem Ipsum is particularly convenient, as it is obviously not intended to be the final text. However, there are times when you might want to include a note prior to your placeholder text that explains what type of text is intended; that is, "The description of the product should go here. Lorem ipsum dolor…"

One potential text-based limitation to consider is how much text you will require, or how much is allowed. The databases that store the data collected from an input field can have character count limits. This may have an impact on the size you make your input fields. It's always a good idea to check with the development team to see if there are any limits and adjust the interface to match what those limits are.

Category pages

As we look back at our site map, we can see that we need to define seven category pages. We will follow the same process used to generate wireframes for the home page. We create a layout that will contain a rough estimate of the text and other content that we think will be required to support the tasks on the page. We will work with the writer and client later to refine these details.

However, there is one big difference: since the category pages span seven different categories, we need to shift our effort slightly to consider the patterns that will work across them all. We could create seven uniquely designed pages if we wanted to, but there really is very little value in doing this. Instead, we will attempt to create a single page template that will work for all seven product categories. This should make the website easier to navigate, and easier to build.

The following is an illustration of the evolution of the category page from our initial sketch to a cleaned up but rudimentary wireframe, and finally becoming a higher fidelity wireframe with actual text and perhaps some icons or graphics:

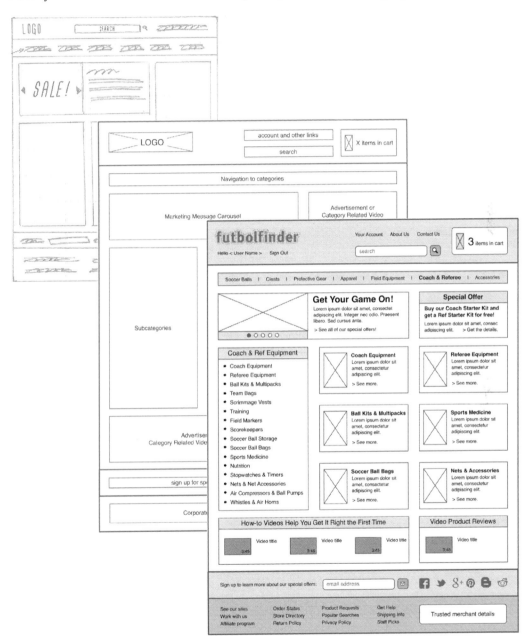

The purpose of the category page is mostly to show products available in that category. To do this, we opted for a three-column grid. This seemed optimized to display many products in a compact space. However, we could have just as easily selected a list view or even just a page of large product images. We discuss these options with the client during the brainstorming session and attempt to quickly narrow down our options with quick exploratory sketches.

The hierarchy of categories is another thing we have to consider. If we had a larger number of items available for purchase on the website, we would have likely needed to add another layer of subcategories. This would help divide the large list of available products into more manageable sets, making it easier for the user to browse through.

Though this wireframe lays out the content and structure of a single category page, it will become the template that we will use for all of them. We will still need to create wireframes for each of the seven category pages in an effort to illustrate the varying text and graphics needed for each of them. However, we can save a great deal of effort and increase the consistency of the experience by reusing the layout pattern illustrated here.

Product detail page

Our product category pages will lead the customer to the product detail pages. Here they will be able to see all of the details and information regarding each product we sell on the website. This will include photos of the product, the title of the item, description, price, reviews, ratings, and other relevant information.

If it is important for our category pages to all utilize the same layout, it is essential that our product detail pages do as well. Since there were only seven category pages, we could offer some unique options for each if we wanted to. Our product detail pages though should be completely based on a single design template. All of the content will be pulled from the database. Nothing will be custom generated. It is important that we define the content patterns that can be applied to all the products sold on the website.

As with the home page and category pages, our brainstorming session with the client yielded enough detail for us to start wireframing a general solution for these templates. With a few more conversations and working sessions with the writer and client, we were able to evolve the content and layout to something a bit more mature.

Here's how our product detail page template has evolved:

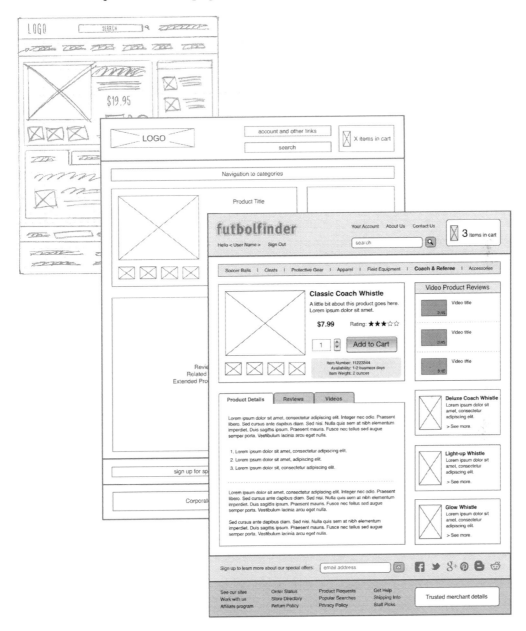

The ability to add the item to the shopping cart is of particular importance to the success of any e-commerce website. It is important that the **Add to Cart** button resides next to the product details "above the fold", which means that it will be seen without the need to scroll the window.

Shopping cart

Following the process used on the other pages we sketched, wireframe the shopping cart with a progressive evolution of detail as shown in the following figure:

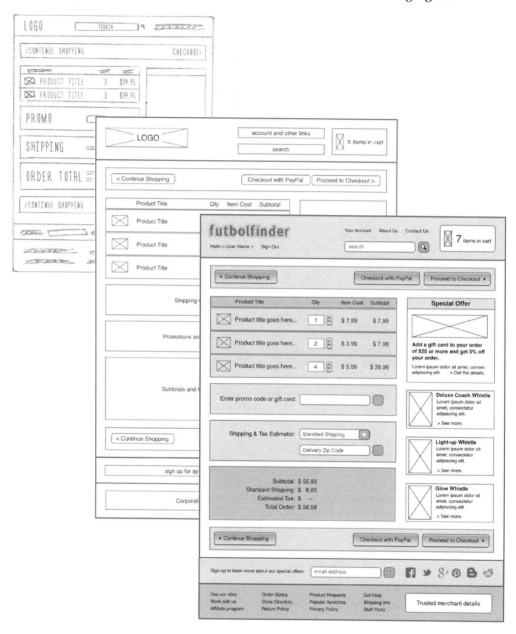

The pages needed for the checkout process will of course need to contain the product and shipping details. We will need to explain the transaction in enough detail to make the customer comfortable about making the purchase. We will need to give the customer the estimated or actual shipping costs. We will also need to offer access to our return policies and any payment security details that will ease the customer's concerns. Only then will they feel comfortable entering their credit card information to make the transaction.

That being said, perhaps the most unique design consideration on this page is scalability. The other pages we have designed up to this point are all somewhat contained and controlled when it comes to page content. This page, however, will need to flex to contain a varying amount of data. The shopping cart experience will need to work just as well for the customer who buys one product as it will for the customer who buys 50 different products. We'll need to consider and wireframe a solution for a simple one item purchase that flexes to accommodate a more complex purchase order.

You have a lot more flexibility and freedom when designing content-rich pages than when designing a page like the shopping cart. Larger online companies have teams dedicated to getting the checkout process perfect and keeping it that way. The conversion of a shopper to a customer all happens on this page. Abandoned virtual shopping carts are a real problem for e-commerce websites. You should educate your client if they don't already know of the significance of making this page usable and intuitive.

Video library page

Our research indicated that including a video library of product reviews and soccer tutorials would offer a lot of value to the customer. We have a lot of freedom to explore creative ways to display this video content. However, the thing to consider is how we will get this type of content. If it is to be pulled from existing video sites like YouTube, the creation of this type of page should be fairly straightforward. On the other hand, if we would like to offer the ability for a user to upload their content to the website directly, the process might get a lot more complicated.

Allowing the user to upload their own content will require a complete set of content management tools. It will require considerations to moderate and delete inappropriate content. It will also require a method to upload and categorize uploaded content, and much more. As we start the wireframing process, it is not uncommon to find a seemingly innocuous feature has become a huge monster that will require a massive amount of time and money to build. When this occurs, we will need to counsel with our client as soon as possible to educate them on the amount of work this feature will actually incur. It might be worth building despite the effort. The client will have to make that decision, and they can only do that once they have the details.

Our media library portion of the website is starting to take shape. We can see the evolution of the idea in the following designs:

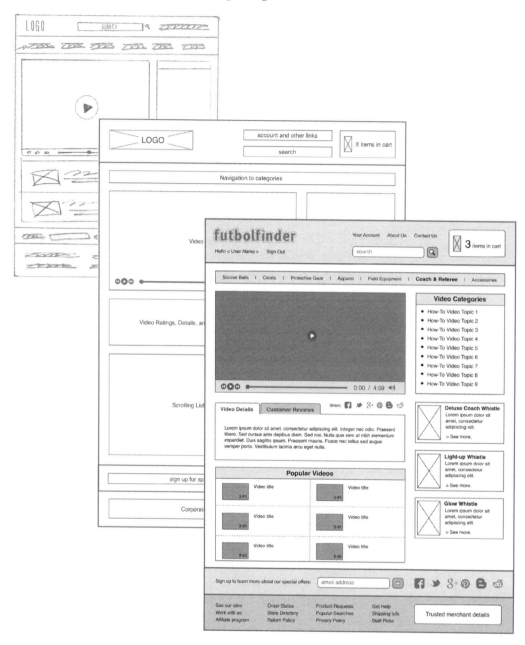

Though we only show a couple of versions of these wireframes, the wireframing process can take several more iterations. The wireframing phase can often be the most intensive and lengthy part of the design process.

Mockups

After working with the client and writer to get the information architecture developed, we will "skin" each page with the visual design layer. This is the part of the design process the client was expecting to start with. By now, it should be clear how much planning and work is needed that most clients haven't factored in to the project plan.

We work through several iterations of each page to apply the visual styling (colors, graphics, fonts, and so on) using the wireframes as a guide.

We will need to explore several possible options for the visual solution. The client will likely request revisions and will approve the final design.

Delivery

Once the mockups have been approved, we move onto cutting out and optimizing the needed images. We speak with the development team to see what they require regarding specification documentation. They may be able to work directly from the mockups and graphic assets we have sent them without the need for further documentation. However, they may require a version of the mockups where the pixel count of the margins and spacing is called out. Image sizes, font faces, font color values, background images, and colors are also elements that will need to be defined for them.

At this point, we need to ensure that we have done everything we can to explain the expected interactions and task flow to the development team. Failure to do this now could lead to some significant variations from the designs we created. At this point in the process, we will likely have talked through every minute detail of the functionality with the stakeholder and other team members. Even though we have spent days and even weeks refining our designs to illustrate this functionality, they will likely not contain every answer to every question that had been discussed.

We should plan on setting up a hand off meeting with the development team to walk through the flow charts and mockups we have created, and include any other documentation that has been generated to support the feature development that has been discussed.

Including a member of the development team in our feature discussions and design reviews can make this transition much smoother. If we don't, we may find that we are walking through every decision that has been made and reopening discussions that had been resolved, primarily because they were not included in the decision-making process.

Reviewing the development efforts

Our efforts on this project are finalized by reviewing the work completed by the development staff. As mentioned earlier, this review is our chance to ensure that the finished product matches our designs in both form and function. It is easy to let this go and not follow up. By the time the development staff is ready for a review of their work, we will have moved onto another project. Our focus will be elsewhere, and they are not always eager to have someone come in and tell them where they went wrong. We need to set the expectation from the start that this review will need to take place and that we expect the stakeholders to be there with us comparing the developed website with the final mockups.

With our design review and subsequent list of update requests resolved, we can consider our work on this project complete.

Summary

As we can see from this example project, the process of wireframing a website is all about evolving an idea from a simple list of features, to a map of pages, to what particular content should be placed on those pages. Each revision adds detail and structure to the design. Eventually, our wireframes are dialed in enough to apply the visual design and graphics to them. It is a crafting process that requires many different participants and a lot of planning and coordination. In the next chapter, we will have a look at an example design project for a mobile device.

3

Example Project – Mobile Device Application

Now that we have seen the design process in action, let's apply the design process to an example design project for a mobile device.

Imagine that during the research phase of the project with our last client, `futbolfinder.com`, we found that they really needed something to help with the marketing of their store to maintain a competitive edge. Many ideas were brainstormed with the marketing team, such as online advertising and search engine optimization. However, the one idea that captured everyone's interest was the creation of an application for a mobile device that would be of particular interest to their target market. The competitive analysis performed earlier showed that a couple of other larger sporting good companies had made similar attempts. However, they were rated very low, and didn't appear to offer a compelling reason for the customer to download and install the app. It would appear that they might be able to set themselves apart from their competition if they offered an application that their target market found useful, and which in turn offered advertising opportunities.

In this chapter, we will cover the following topics:

- How to use research techniques to isolate the qualities our primary customers possess, and what product features they might find valuable

- How to filter our initial feature list to define our **Minimum Viable Product (MVP)**

- How to map out the high-level details of how our features might function and knit together

- How to map out the unique screens each user profile will require

- How to define the function and form of each screen of our product through sketches and wireframes
- Some considerations when applying the visual design layer

Research

We have been called in again to help design the user experience. After finding out a bit more about how we work and what we do, the client calls us in from the start and looks to us to guide them through the process of figuring out the features that are needed, the structure and interactions the application will require, the content needed to support the product, and the final visual design.

Stakeholder interview and persona development

We interview the client to find that he really has no idea of what the user might find useful. It looks as though we will need to employ some design techniques that will guide them through an examination of their customers and explore some new ideas.

We set up a project kickoff meeting with the client and key stakeholders to brainstorm the features this application might have. The personas we generated for this client were very useful in the creation of their website. Since this project is aimed at offering value to their existing customer base, we decide that we can reuse these personas for this effort.

Our brainstorming session with the client using personas as a focus for the discussion yields the following results:

SUSAN SOCCERMOM

Age: 36

Location: Charleston, SC

Profession: Mother & Director of family activities

Susan Soccermom represents the segment of users that visit the store due to their children's involvement with a local youth soccer league. She would be interested in knowing about specials and sales on equipment that relate to her children's soccer equipment needs. She is also interested in the game times, locations, and events related to the league and her children's teams. Due to her busy schedule, it can sometimes be a challenge for her to keep track of the game times and locations.

Perhaps the mobile app could help her by obtaining the game schedule and location from the league or coach. In addition to being guided to the location of away games, she could be given advertisements for new products and special sales for youth players.

ERIC ENTHUSIAST

Age: 47

Location: Portland, OR

Profession: High School History Teacher

Eric Enthusiast represents the segment of customers who love to watch soccer games. He doesn't play the game himself, but he tracks his favorite players and team scores and watches as many games as he can. He would love to know about when teams are playing near him and have access to special deals on tickets. If the games were not local, he would also be interested in knowing where he can meet up with his friends to watch the game on TV. He is interested in fan gear and promotional licensed memorabilia. If he has access to crazy wigs and face paint in his team's colors, he might just buy them if the price is right.

Perhaps the mobile app could help him by giving him a schedule of the games his favorite teams are playing and access to purchase tickets online. We could pull in scores, stats, and news updates about his favorite teams/players so he can keep track of their performance. We could also offer specific promotions for the type of products he would likely purchase from the store.

PETER PLAYER

Age: 20

Location: Denver, CO

Profession: College Student

Peter Player represents the segment of customers who are a combination of an enthusiast, player, and coach. Peter would be interested in much of the same things as the other two from both a feature and product perspective. He might also be interested in instructional content to help his youth soccer coaching activities. This may also influence his shopping habits. He'll likely be more interested in products related to refereeing and field equipment.

Perhaps the mobile app could offer coaches special deals on certain product categories that are a bit more targeted to their needs. It could offer a management portal for coaches and league officials to enter the schedule and location of games. This could then be shared with the team members and families.

Weighing features

Once we have all of the ideas captured, we review with the team the viability of options by running them through the Feature Reality Test that was discussed in *Chapter 2, Example Project – E-commerce Website*. We examine our personas to see which has the highest potential impact on the success of the company. We also identify which feature set has the highest likelihood of successfully impacting the user's life in a positive way.

From all the possible options, the team has decided that the customer with the most influence and purchasing power is **Susan Soccermom**. Though coming to the store looking for a bargain, Susan represents the largest group of shoppers with a predictable and perennial need. Basically put, children in youth soccer leagues need equipment to play the game safely. Furthermore, they will likely outgrow their equipment each season. This means there is a very high likelihood that the customer base Susan represents will need to purchase new equipment at the beginning of every new season.

Creating an app with features which will make her life easier will keep her using it. Every time she uses the app, we can remind her of where she can find the soccer gear her child needs to play safely. Not only that, the app can bring special deals and sales to her attention. Everybody wins!

Focusing on Susan's needs for her child's youth soccer league also touches on the coaching needs of Peter Player. It would appear that focusing on features that apply to local soccer leagues is the most predictable path for success and will likely offer the largest return on their investment.

Using this research and analysis, the team agrees on a phased approach for developing this application. They will pursue the following versions.

Version 1 will focus on the scheduling needs of **Susan Soccermom** as well as the coaching needs of **Peter Player**. The agreed upon features are as follows:

- Ability to access the schedules and maps to all games
- Ability to view/e-mail the people of the team on the roster
- Ability to invite others to download/install the app
- Ability to enter and display scores of games
- Ability to offer advertising for related products and special offers

Version 2 of the product could expand to meet the needs of **Eric Enthusiast**:

- Pro team schedules
- Notifications of game times
- Ability to purchase tickets
- Local places to watch the game
- Sales and special offers for licensed team apparel

 It is important to consider a versioned solution when defining a product. Our MVP should only contain the most basic features that are required to make the app work in its simplest form. Adding too many features in our initial product can delay our app's entry into the marketplace. The added complexity of too many features can often kill our product before it gets out the door. It can be worthwhile, for quality and stability's sake, to observe and refine our initial offering before we add more complexity to it.

Information Architecture

There is more work we could do during the research phase, but we have an initial list of realistic features and a clear goal of what the product has to offer the end user. Since the product seems realistic and the team is in alignment with the objective, it is time to start mapping out the details of how these features might work and knit together.

Interaction maps

We start by creating an interaction map to illustrate how users will access these features and how the user navigates through the application. This flowchart is very similar to the site map we created for the website, though it will likely be a little more complex, and will focus a bit more on task flow; the path a user must follow to complete any given objective. We will ignore some of that complexity in our first map. Our goal will be to start capturing the high-level details.

Similar to the MVP concept mentioned previously, it is important to start with simplicity in mind. Perhaps the most difficult part of this process is learning to avoid digging too deep into the details at the start. If we aim at having multiple versions of this map in advance, it might be easier to avoid the trap of getting bogged down by too much information. Start by documenting concepts and high-level tasks rather than specifics and plan on adding the finer details later.

Our first map

In this case, we start by quickly mapping out the mechanics of how the user will be introduced to the product. We know they will download and install the application on their phone. When they start it for the first time, they will first see a splash screen that will usually display the logo and possibly the version number for a few seconds. They will then need to create an account or sign in if they already have one. We can offer a quick tutorial if it will help the user understand how to navigate the application.

At this point, the path the user will follow will depend upon how they were introduced to the application itself. If they found the application on their own, they will need to locate the team or league they belong to and join it. If they were sent an invitation from a league representative, coach, or another parent or player, they will be taken directly to the team page they were invited to. The experience I just explained with text should become a map that looks something like this:

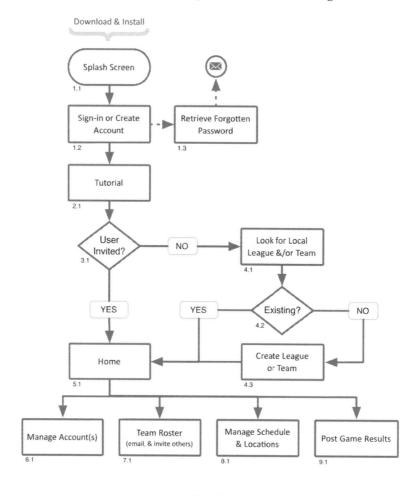

We should note that our aim as UX designers is to find the best interface solution possible. To accomplish this, we will need to start by exploring various options. Inexperienced designers will often leap too quickly to adopt a solution before accounting for all of the details. They then end up assuming a defensive posture in meetings when problems with the UX logic are exposed. We should be wary of situations where we have to defend our work too much, or if we find ourselves getting emotional or frustrated. It usually means that we just didn't think through everything we should have, or perhaps there was some data we didn't have access to.

We should attempt to keep our minds open when this happens (and it will happen). We do ourselves no favor by staunchly defending a solution that is not comprehensive. Sometimes we have to back up and try again. This is especially true when new features are added to the project, or when unexpected complexities are found in a particular task flow. I am of the opinion that if we define and consider all the details, a true and proper solution will materialize for us. Adopt the process of proposing a solution and inviting the team to punch holes in it by exposing UX snarls that negatively affect the experience. This invitation of criticism will help keep us from getting defensive, help us refine the experience, and will assist us in obtaining team alignment and buy-in with the final UX strategy.

Our refined map

For our second version of the interaction map, we expand it to illustrate the task flow followed by each user type. Parents/players, coaches, and league representatives will each have different objectives and tasks. Three different colored lines have represented the path of those tasks.

With these different users in mind, we find that we need to add several management pages for the coach and league representatives. These pages will let them invite new team members as well as delete or edit other roster details. They will require a means of managing the game schedule and locations. If we offer the ability to upload photos and comments about the games, then we will also likely need to offer a means of moderating that content. We can offer those privileges to the league representative, coach, assistant coach, and even the parents and players themselves.

We add all of these features to our map, and it evolves into this:

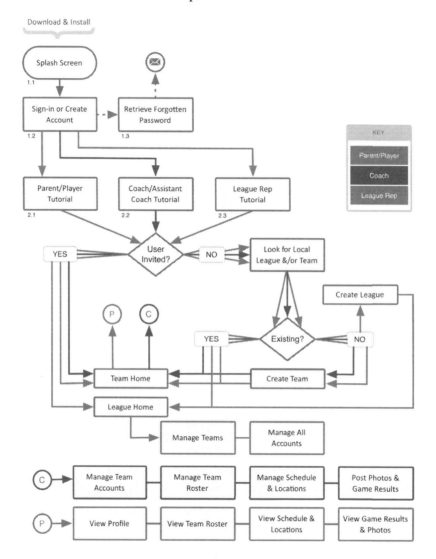

There are many different ways to interpret this data into shapes. Take the **Sign-in** section shown at point **1.2** in the preceding figure. That could be represented as a decision point using a diamond shape. As in, do we want to sign in or create a new account? We could also use a parallelogram to represent that data is being input into the system. It all depends upon the level of detail we require. Since the focus of this particular chart is to examine the task flow, not account management, we will just label it as a manual process. It's not entirely accurate, but to show it in more detail would bog down the message we are attempting to get across.

Sketches and mockups

We have vetted our interaction maps with the team and they have agreed on the overall task flow defined for the various user types. These are: parent, player, coach, and league representative. We will use our **Susan Soccermom** persona to represent the parents and players using the application. We will use our **Eric Enthusiast** persona to represent the coach and possibly the league representative user types.

As we add more detail to the experience, we may find the league representative's tasks are unique enough to justify the creation of a persona to represent that specific user type.

When in this type of situation, we will need to make a judgment call on when technique-like persona generation is helpful and when it will slow down the process. I have seen designers who are very thorough about using such techniques. Though it takes time and effort, it can pay off in the end. Accounting for all possible scenarios will likely mean fewer revisions.

There is not a 100 percent correct answer for this. We will need to account for the needs of the product, as well as the pace of the team, and refine our approach depending on those circumstances.

For this project, let's say the team agrees to utilize the personas we have already generated to represent our user types. Now we move onto the next step in the Information Architecture phase, the creation of mockups.

We start by sketching the different pages shown in our interaction maps. While drawing out the details, we include notes about navigational decisions, observations about potential areas of confusion, and questions that we'll need to answer later on.

Creating a new account

The following figure shows our sketch, and eventual wireframe, of the interface to create a new account. Since asking for too much personal information can cause people to abandon the account creation process, we pare down our list of required data to only the essentials.

The experience should be fairly quick and painless by asking for the user's name and e-mail address. We'll also ask for the user's zip code to assist in locating their league or team from our database. This should be enough personal information to get started and is light enough to not scare them away. We'll capture any other data we need as they get more invested in the application and use more of its features.

We can gather credit card information within the store's checkout process. Other personal information can be collected when the user joins a team and is added to the roster, or becomes a coach or league representative.

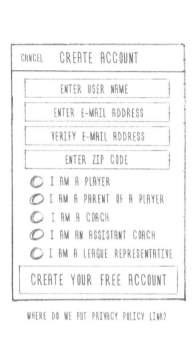

Please keep in mind that there are laws requiring us to communicate our intentions regarding the usage of personal information in a privacy policy. We will likely be required to include other policies such as a "terms of use" policy, and possibly an **End Users Licensing Agreement (EULA)**. These need to be made available when the user creates their account, and will need to be made available within the product as well. Since the user will require a page to manage their profile and account information entered on this page and elsewhere, we'll plan on including access to these policies there as well.

Now that we have our initial account creation page defined, let's move onto the next step in the user experience.

Finding your team

This sketch and wireframe show the follow-up step that occurs once we have created a new account. If the user was invited, they will skip this step as the system will know exactly what league and/or team they were invited to. If the user was not invited, the application takes the zip code entered during the account creation process and presents a list of leagues and teams that are nearby. This is represented by block 4.1 in the interaction map. If the user cannot find the league or team they belong to in the list, chances are they haven't been created yet. The button at the bottom of the page will let anyone start defining a team. They may then send out invitations to other parents, players, and league representatives to install the app and join the team roster. Selecting the "League Rep" account type will offer the ability to create and manage leagues and multiple teams.

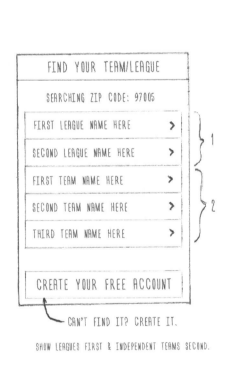

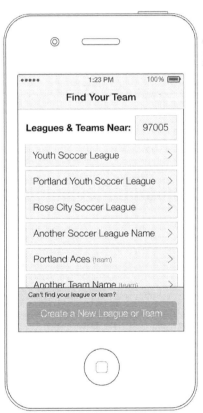

It's natural to discover elements and features we didn't account for in our flowcharts as we dig into the wireframe details. The more thorough we are while developing our interaction maps, the fewer revisions we'll have to make later on.

Here are a few things to consider when sketching out our initial wireframing thoughts on paper. You may notice that my sketches are slightly inaccurate and, well, messy. I know many designers who have purchased stencils, rulers, and templates to help make their sketches look more professional and presentable. I too have tried this, but found it to be counterproductive. When sketches look too clean or beautiful they become precious. There is a natural desire, especially in designers, to protect precious things. Since this step in the process is all about quickly examining and abandoning ideas until you find those that work, this preciousness can slow you down and hamper your ability to think beyond your perfect sketches. I would encourage you to make them loose, fluid, and fast. Making your sketches on a whiteboard can be a good way to avoid this scenario, and makes it easier to involve others in the discussion.

The following wireframes show how the process will continue for the user who locates their league and team.

Joining a team

The user who locates their team without an invitation will be able to join the team by clicking on the button that says "**Join This Team**" at the bottom of the screen. We can give the coach or league representative the ability to approve requests to join a team if added security is desired. The decision to offer this will need to be agreed upon by the team. And, if needed, the functionality will need to be added to the interaction map. The ability to monitor these requests will need to be added to the coach and league representative management screens.

This brings us to a common scenario when designing the task flow for such interfaces. We can either offer instant access to the team or send an approval request to the coach or website administrator. Instant access requires the least amount of interface, but is also the least secure. Since we are dealing with children's contact information, we'll likely want to restrict access to only those who are approved. Because of this, we'll likely need to create a system later on in the project that will let the administrator manage those requests.

There is one other common solution in these situations. We can offer an option in the administrator's control panel that will let them define whether they would like to manage these access requests or not. This is the most flexible option, but as you might expect, flexibility almost always increases complexity. This is another situation where we'll need to examine the user's needs and make a judgment call on what is most appropriate. We'll also want to ensure that we include the development team in the discussion. Very often, adding features like this can add a significant amount of development time to the schedule. If our proposal is too costly, we may need to brainstorm another solution with the development team. Once agreed upon, we'll need to update our interaction maps and wireframes with our new feature.

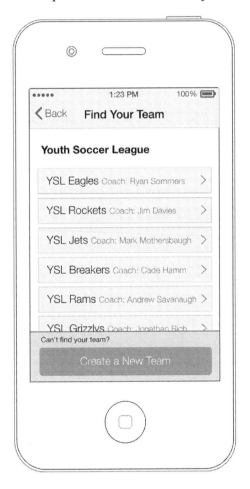

Your team's home page

Once the user has located and joined their team, they will be taken to the team home page. This page will become the default landing page anytime they open the application. Considerations may need to be explored to account for parents who use this application to track the games of multiple children.

We can see from the following figure that there are a lot of options to consider regarding possible content and features for the team home page. We have included access points to the coach and team's contact information, the maps to the games, notifications, and a few other things.

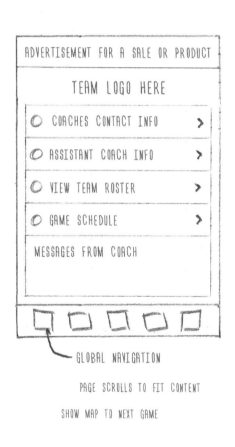

Navigation options

Page content isn't the only thing that needs to be carefully considered. The navigation model we choose to employ can have a monumental impact on the usability of our application. It is important to understand the options at our disposal and their associated pros and cons.

There are many commonly used styles, and an almost infinite number of navigational options we could dream up. That being said, when it comes to navigational schemas, there are really only two paradigms to choose from. Our options are to employ a **portal navigation** model or a **global navigation** model.

Portal navigation

The portal navigation model consists of a primary portal page that contains all the navigational access points to every tool or task in the website or application. We move from this page to the tool or feature we wish to use, and when done, we must return to the portal to select another one. This model usually requires navigational links known as "breadcrumbs" that will lead us back up the trail of navigation we travelled down. Mobile device applications that use this model often have to rely on the use of many back buttons to return us to the main portal or index. This is often caused by the amount of space breadcrumb trails take up, which is not always compatible with the limited screen space mobile devices offer.

The portal model can be seen in the sketches and wireframes of the store portion of this example found in the next section. The home page of the store contains the access points to all of the product categories. I opted for a **breadcrumb navigation** model rather than back buttons to return the user to the portal page. The breadcrumb navigation looks like this:

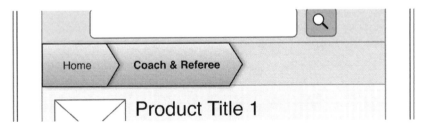

Global navigation

The global navigation model consists of a set of navigational links that are shown on nearly every page of the website or application. This is usually shown in a **nav bar** or row on navigational links/access points. This prevents the need to use breadcrumb navigation or back buttons. The user can simply click on whatever feature they want to go to at any point.

As illustrated in the following figure, you can see we chose to use a global navigation model for the team- and league-related screens in our application:

When to remove navigation

Regardless of the model chosen, the navigation (portal or global) is usually removed when the user is working on a task that spans multiple screens, or that follows a specific and rigid set of steps. The navigation will return once they have completed their task, or have cancelled out of the process.

The typical e-commerce checkout process is a good example of this. When a customer has added items to their cart and is attempting to make their purchase, it is best to reduce the number of navigational links that will lead them away from that experience. Retaining the navigation options used elsewhere in the store will not only complicate the experience by adding more content to the page, but it is also counterproductive to our ultimate goal of completing the sale. Offer the user several links out of the checkout process and they will be more likely to abandon their shopping session.

In addition to the checkout process, we will likely want to remove the navigation on tasks that require multiple screens or pages to be completed. If the user is midway through entering their data and they navigate away from the page, we'll need to stop the experience and ask them if they are leaving intentionally. It's often easier to reduce the number of links that lead away from the task at hand. They will either need to complete their task or expressly choose to cancel it to return to a screen that has the navigational links.

The Futbol Finder storefront

Up to this point, we have been addressing the needs and desires of the end user. Now let's examine the reason the application has been created by our client. They need a way to bring customers into the store. They could have spent their advertising budget on traditional media. Instead, they opted for an application that would offer a service to their existing and potential customers, which would allow them to advertise directly to their target market in a more controlled way.

The following sketches and wireframes will explore the Futbol Finder store as found in the application we have been developing:

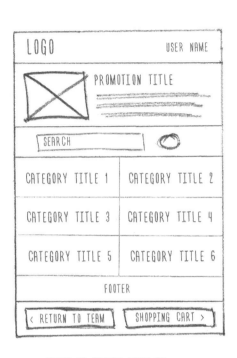

This figure shows a rough sketch and subsequent wireframe of the mobile device version of the store's home page. This storefront is accessed from the team- and league-related pages in two ways. The first is a direct link to the store's home page that resides on the right-hand side of the global navigation bar. The other access point takes the form of an advertising banner that resides at the top of the screen on the league and team tracker portion of the application. This banner lets the client advertise special offers and sales, which can take the user directly to a product detail page or some other promotional page.

Once the user has entered the store, the experience changes significantly. The navigation paradigm switches from a global model to a portal model, meaning the home page will lead the user to category pages. If they wish to browse to another category, they will need to return to the home page and select another category.

We have included a button at the bottom of the page that will return the user to the team- and league-related pages, but the intent is to keep the user in the store and not offer them too many obvious paths out. The bulk of the navigation in this portion of the app will be focused on guiding them through the store.

Having walked through the design of the website as our first example project, we can see that there is a major difference in the desktop version of the website and the mobile device version. Since the limited screen size reduces the amount of marketing that can be done, we have created a fairly basic storefront that offers stripped down search and browse functionality. The store structure and product taxonomy will remain the same, but we may find that it benefits the user by reducing some of the content and product details to optimize the experience for the reduced screen size of our mobile device.

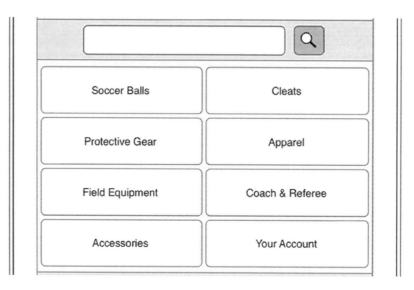

The primary links on the home page will let the user search for specific product keywords or browse the different product categories.

Our next task will be to design the experience for a category page.

Shopping by product category

This particular wireframe shows where the user would be taken if they tapped on the **Coach & Referee** category button on the home page:

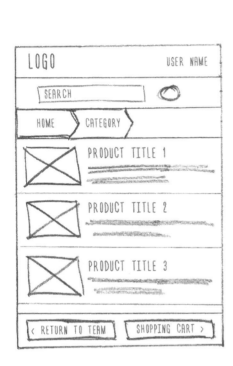
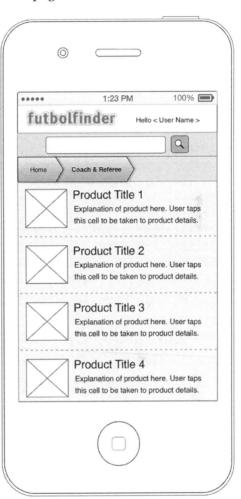

Our wireframe of this category page will be used as a template for our other category pages, just as we did with the website version of the store.

We block out where the product images will reside. This is shown with a simple box on the left-hand side of the screen. We include the product title and some explanatory text for each product. Tapping a product will take the user to the product detail page. Here, we can offer much more information about the product and include reviews, ratings, and other details.

We may wish to explore a few other versions of this page to ensure that we are creating the best possible interface. For instance, instead of adding the first sentence of the product description under the product title, perhaps we could show the price, and let the customer add the item to the cart directly from this category page. We'll still need to add a means of accessing the product detail page, but this alternative solution could possibly slow down the purchase process. After we explore some of these different solutions, we can review them with the client to decide which one we should go with.

Usability testing

This would be the time to start testing our design decisions. This can be as simple as finding a few people we know who match our personas and having them take a look at our wireframes to gauge their reaction. We can create prototypes of our designs or just print them out. We can show them a single wireframe of each interface or display multiple options and let them choose the one they prefer.

The more opinions we receive, the higher the likelihood that we will be giving the customer what they want. We can always guess and make assumptions about what they want, but it's surprising how often we get it wrong. The important thing here will be to get some feedback from people who are likely to use the product before taking our designs to a higher fidelity.

Presenting our deliverables

It is common practice to have a formal review of each round of wireframes with the client or team. To make our work easier to present and understand, we create a document that first contains our interaction map and then the wireframes in an order that guides the audience through the task flow. Including comments about each wireframe is a great way to ensure our thoughts and concerns are accurately communicated.

Most wireframing applications will let us apply links to our pages. We can add a great deal of clarity by linking the cells of our task flow diagram to the wireframes each cell represents. We can add even more clarity by linking the navigation in our wireframes so our presentation becomes a navigable prototype.

Once we have received feedback from the team, we can update our flowcharts and wireframes and prepare a new presentation for our next review. During this iterative process, our goal will be to address all the issues found during the review and increase fidelity by adding text, graphics, and other details. We will continue to work with the client and team to refine these wireframes until all the details and content have been satisfactorily defined.

Summary

Though not able to take us through the entire experience of designing this application, I have touched upon most of the significant processes and patterns we will likely face in nearly all projects we take on.

Throughout this chapter, we selected and employed the research techniques that would help us isolate the qualities our primary customers possess. We used this research to explore potential product features they might find valuable. We filtered our list of features to include only those that would add significant value. We then mapped out the high-level details of how these features might function and fit together, defined the function and form of each screen of our product through sketches and wireframes, tested our designs by getting feedback from potential users, and repeated the process by reviewing and refining our wireframes with the client until all the required details were satisfactorily included in our designs.

We have now reviewed the typical UX design process and have seen it applied to a couple of example projects. Employing the same process to your software design efforts should give you reliably effective results.

That being said, knowing the process is only the beginning. The place to focus your studies and efforts will now turn to learning various design techniques that are commonly used in the design industry. I have walked you through several of them in our example projects, but there are many more to explore. The more of these you become familiar with, the easier it will be for you to find the answers you seek.

The next chapter will get you acquainted with many of the commonly-used research techniques used in the industry today.

4
Research Techniques

The design process described in this book lays out what type of information or level of detail we should be seeking at a particular point in the project. It does not explain how to get the information we need. For this, we rely on various techniques. These are exercises or methodologies that help us ask the appropriate questions and then analyze the answers we receive. These techniques will help us obtain the information we require to ensure our design solutions are on target and offer value to the end user.

I have demonstrated the use of a few of these techniques in the example projects included in this book. However, since each project will require a slightly different approach, and because there are so many options available, it would be impractical to find an example that would adequately illustrate them all. Instead, I will use the next two chapters to supply descriptions of several of the more commonly used techniques which we need to familiarize ourselves with. There has been much written about these methodologies that is worth researching further. An experienced UX designer will know most of these and many other techniques, and should know when it is appropriate to employ them.

Commonly used, effective research techniques

Here is a very brief description of several methodologies aimed at helping us get the answers we seek during the research phase of a project. There are many others, and there will be many more developed as the software design industry continues to mature. I would recommend searching the Internet or other related books for more implementation details and examples of their usage.

Stakeholder interviews

Getting the project details from the primary stakeholders is likely the first thing we will need to do to get started on any project. The list of potential questions can be quite long. However, they usually roll up under one of the following primary questions:

- Who is going to use this software or site?
- What tasks does the user wish to accomplish?
- What does the maker of the software or site wish to accomplish?
- What technology will be used? (Are there any limitations to consider?)
- Why would the public use your software or site over another?
- What content will be needed to support the user in accomplishing their goals?

If we are redesigning an existing site or application, we will likely find it valuable to seek answers to these additional questions:

- What features or complexities are hampering or otherwise negatively affecting the existing user experience?
- What additional features would the user or publisher find helpful in the next version of the product?

Design tenet scorecard

Design tenets are a list of the primary design attributes or qualities that are valued by the company or client we are working with. These attributes can describe the quality of interaction, visual style, tone of the text-based content, or even qualities that are a bit more technical in nature. Simply put, they can be anything that we would like to see represented in every interface we create.

Here is an example scorecard:

Design Tenet Scorecard	n/a	Absent	Poor	Good	Perfect
Discoverable			✔		
Intuitive & Learnable			✔		
Obvious Task Flow		✔			
Well Crafted, Modern, and Fresh					✔
Low Step Count to Accomplish Each Task					✔
Engaging, Vibrant, and Fun					✔
Scalable				✔	

When there is misalignment on the vision or execution of a product or interface, it can be extremely helpful to put these tenets in the form of a scorecard. We then use this to grade the interface we have created against each design tenet. More often than not, one or more of the design tenets will have been neglected or entirely absent from the interface. Including this examination in our design reviews can help turn a general sense of dissatisfaction with a particular design solution into a focused discussion about specific attributes that need to be improved.

This example scorecard is one that I recently created and used with a client. I managed to get everyone involved with the product development in the same room to quickly brainstorm what the company's design values were. Together, we defined seven design tenets or attributes that were desired in every interface we created. The idea being that if each of these values were adequately represented, we would have a higher likelihood of obtaining the company's goals. We would have a higher likelihood of producing a product that successfully gave the customer what they needed.

I realize that this might seem to be of little value. After all, the tenets we have listed are all things that we should be striving for all of the time. However, each company will have a unique set of design attributes that they value above all others. There's a very good chance that they will not match our own personal values. So, it is important to understand what they are from the start so we can deliver a solution that matches their expectations. If we don't understand their values, we will design with our own values in mind. That doesn't always satisfy the client.

Understanding the client's values may also help us understand where we need to educate them regarding the possible negative effects their particular values could have on the experience.

For instance, let's say our client says they really appreciate new cutting edge interfaces. They like inventing new ways of solving problems with their software. They also say that they like clean interfaces that are not bogged down with a lot of help content or explanations. In this scenario, we can point to a potential conflict that might arise with this combination of values. We can explain that without some sort of tutorial content for this new interface, we may find we have a lot of users who just don't understand how the product is intended to work.

The example scorecard I have included here offered significant value during the wireframing process of the project I was working on. The project started out fine, but I started to receive requests from one team member who thought the interface should be less guided and much more freeform. His desire for less navigation and guidance conflicted with the previously documented design tenet that stated that the product should include an "obvious task flow".

Utilizing the scorecard, I was able to pinpoint where his requests were conflicting with the design attributes established by the team. It helped explain the logic of the design decisions I had made. And, it put the onus on him to justify his request with the knowledge that it was out of alignment with the team's prescribed values. In the end, it saved us a lot of time and effort. We were better able to focus on attributes of value and avoid going in directions that ran counter to those values.

Competitive analysis

Examining similar applications, sites, or products is a reliable way to quickly determine how much work is needed to compete in the existing marketplace. This exercise entails crawling through each product to examine and document the following:

- Product features of value
- Each product's target market
- What they do right and where they fail
- New ideas and features that will help offer a better experience

Creating a summary of this research will help us create a plan to meet or exceed the competition. Reviewing the results of this research with the team and following up the review with a brainstorming session is a very effective way to kick-start some new ideas.

Though our ultimate plan is to create something new that completely revolutionizes the marketplace, we often have to start by getting a simple v1 product into the marketplace. This is commonly referred to as the **MVP** or **Minimum Viable Product**. This means the product contains only those features that are essential for it to function in its most basic form.

It can be easy to get caught up in the fervor to design something that beats out the competition with our initial release. There are times when this can be done. However, it is often smarter to promote a feature roadmap that plans out the evolution of our product through multiple versioned releases.

As designers, we will likely need to help define how the experience will evolve through these multiple releases. We'll want to ensure that features are released in an order that will make sense to the user, and will always maintain the usability and integrity of the product.

Personas and user profiles

As illustrated in *Chapter 1*, *The Design Process*, personas are invented avatars that represent a certain segment of our end users. Using personas during the design process is a very common means of gaining an understanding of what typical customers or users look like. They do an amazing job of helping the team focus their efforts on what a particular user might need. Without them, it's easy to unknowingly have the team examine the interface from the point of view of different users. This can cause disagreement regarding what a particular interface needs to include to appropriately serve its end user.

This is an easy trap to fall into. Several years ago, I found myself in this situation. I was presenting some new product designs with a co-worker. The product was addressing some very complex task flows that were not easy for a novice user to understand. A disagreement sprung up about how we were handling some of the details in the experience. After a couple of hours going back and forth about why the interface succeeded or failed, we finally figured out that we were thinking of two entirely different users. My teammate was looking at the designs through the eyes of an admin or expert user. I was attempting to design with the inexperienced user in mind.

Once I understood the point of view through which he was examining the interface, I was able to adequately address his concerns by showing him the admin task flow we had previously created. The user he had in mind was actually never going to see the interface we had been reviewing.

This was a costly misunderstanding that caused frustration and wasted a lot of time. Had we been using our persona's names during our conversation, it would've become obvious that we were thinking about two entirely different user profiles.

Creating personas

The process of creating personas starts with researching what types of users are expected to use the application or site you are creating. A quick brainstorming session with the team should be enough to get a list and description of these user types. As we examine the potential users in our list, it's common to find that we have many user types that are very similar. We'll want to consolidate those down to a number that is easy to remember by creating a representative for multiple user types.

Here's an example of what this might look like. As we can see from the following example, our list of potential users is too long to be useful. 18 different user types are far too many to remember. We really need to narrow this down to something more manageable. I can't really give an ideal number of personas to develop. It will depend largely on the product. However, I would say it is common to have somewhere between three to six different personas.

As illustrated in this example, we were able to consolidate our 18 possible user profiles down to six personas. Each one represented a group of users with what we deemed to be redundant similarities:

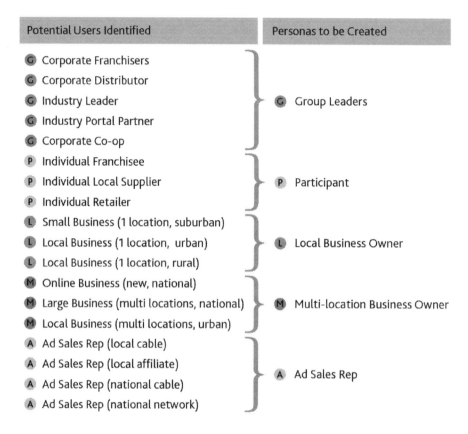

Once we have our representatives, we'll want to start creating a personality for each persona that uniquely identifies them. Even their name should match their personality to make them more memorable. For instance, if the persona is a student, then perhaps their name could be something like Laura Learner. If the persona is a carpenter, perhaps a name like Harold Hammer would help us remember who he is.

Many designers love to add a ton of detail to their personas. The belief is, the more you know about that user, the more you will understand their needs and wants. However, I've found that this added detail tends to get lost. From my experience, it's generally sufficient to include:

- A memorable name
- A photo
- A quote that represents the attitude of the persona

- Where they are from

- Their profession

- How much they earn a year

- A short description of their family life

- A few hobbies

- A brief summary of their level of experience

- A description of their objective when it comes to using the site or application

We might find value in adding details such as the languages they speak, the features they require, and/or special product-related concerns they may have. The list of options is endless. We'll need to examine our product and users to define the unique list of attributes that will best differentiate them from one another.

After these personas have been created, we need a way to keep them in the minds of our co-workers during the design and development process. Creating posters of each persona that you can hang on the office walls or cards of each that you can leave on the conference table can help everyone remember who they are.

 There are many more techniques and methods we can use to help generate personas. And, there are even more that will help improve their adoption rate by your team. I would recommend searching the Internet for "UX personas" to find more details and instruction.

Heuristic evaluation

A heuristic evaluation is the examination of an existing product to see how well it works and to gauge where it can be improved. From my experience, this requires some understanding of the existing best practices for the design industry. For instance, when evaluating the login screen of an existing site or application, it is common and likely necessary for that screen to contain: a place to enter the user's name or e-mail address, a place to enter their password, a link to the terms of service, and a link to the privacy policy. It may also need to contain a link to help content if the user experiences problems, appropriate success or error messaging, notification of which fields are required, the ability to either create an account or sign in with an existing account, as well as a secure means of retrieving a forgotten password.

This evaluation will require us to crawl through the entire site or application documenting what was executed well and what requires improvement or a full redesign. We then follow up with suggestions about what needs to be done to improve the problems we have pointed out.

As we document and eventually present our findings to our client, it is important to remember to be kind. We don't want to be overly bold or critical of the flaws that we have found. Offending our client at this stage will likely be counterproductive. However, honesty is critical to the evaluation's integrity. Creating a scorecard for each area of examination can help pinpoint the areas of concern, while allowing you to also show what is in good shape.

Here is an example of what a scorecard for the account creation or sign-in process might look like:

1. Account Creation/Sign In	n/a	Absent (score: 0)	Poor (score: 1)	Good (score: 2)	Perfect (score: 3)
Ability to create new or sign into existing account			✔		
Required fields are clearly designated		✔			
Error messaging is present and helpful			✔		
Success messaging is present and clear					✔
Secure means of retrieving password is present					✔
Privacy policy information is available				✔	
Terms of service information is available		✔			
Related help content is available		✔			
Overall Score	1.25	(Average score: 2 Perfect score: 3)			

 Searching for "UX Heuristic Evaluation Techniques" should direct you to further details and resources that will help you complete a successful heuristic evaluation.

Card sorting

Card sorting is a commonly used technique used to organize product taxonomies, navigational categories, and other lists that require sorting into logical groups. The process is quite simple. We write the name of every object on a card, place the cards randomly on a table or stick them on a wall, and then ask people to sort the cards into logical groupings. Not everyone will sort the cards quite the same way. However, if we get enough people to do it, we will likely see a common pattern emerge. This common sorting is generally what we will adopt as our solution.

 Searching for "Card Sorting Techniques" on Google should lead you to more details and instructions on how to hold a successful card-sorting session with your team.

Focus groups

Focus groups are a very common and well-used research technique. Historically used by marketing professionals, it can also be used by software designers to gauge interest in proposed features, or just to seek out what ideas current or potential users have.

This technique involves getting several existing users, or potential users of our product, into a room for a group brainstorming session. A member of the software team usually moderates the session to keep it on track. There can be a script of feature-related questions, but it can be very freeform in nature.

The success of these sessions can really depend on the quality of the participants. It is critical to involve participants who accurately represent your target market. Get the wrong participants and your session can go off course and will end up being a waste of time and money.

There are companies that can help find appropriately targeted focus group participants. However, you may find that you need to send out invites to your users or post an invite to related online forums.

If done right, focus groups can really help define your feature list. It takes the guesswork out, allowing you to move forward confidently and quickly.

 Searching for "How to run a UX-based focus group" should offer more resources and instruction on how to set up and complete a successful focus group.

User surveys

User surveys entail sending product- and feature-related questionnaires to users or potential users of an existing product. Think of this as a variation on the focus group concept. We can get feedback on proposed interface mockups or prototypes, as well as gauge interest of new features being considered for the next version of the product.

Though not as interactive as a focus group, it has some pretty significant advantages. It can be much easier and cost effective to enact user surveys over focus groups. We avoid the expense and scheduling issues experienced when attempting to get a targeted group of people into a specific location at a specific time. Furthermore, we have the potential of sending our surveys out to thousands of people, thus adding the potential to significantly increase the veracity of our results.

There are several survey services available online that assist in the creation, distribution, and aggregation of survey results.

 Searching for "online survey tools" should give us several options to choose from. Popular options include:

- Survey Monkey (www.surveymonkey.com)
- Client Heartbeat (www.clientheartbeat.com)
- Survey Gizmo (www.surveygizmo.com)

Brainstorming

Perhaps the most significant and valuable technique we can employ during the research phase is holding brainstorming sessions with the stakeholders and other members of the team.

Depending upon your personality, brainstorming can sometimes be a scary proposition. You may not particularly enjoy being the one leading group discussions. There are also situations where others may take this open request for ideas as their opportunity to take control of the project direction and design process you are attempting to promote. In these situations in particular, I've found it is important to follow these guidelines:

- You should schedule the meeting and directly invite the participants.
- Assign a note taker in advance so you are free to lead the meeting. The note taker should be asked to send their notes to the group directly after the meeting.
- Start the meeting by stating the objective of the brainstorming session. Share the research you have completed to date in an attempt to get everyone on the same page.

- You should be an active participant in the discussion. Help sketch out the ideas that evolve during the discussion on a whiteboard or large sketchpad.

- Attempt to keep everyone discussing the topic at hand by placing tangential topics on a list of items to discuss at a later time.

- Wrap up your meeting by restating who has takeaway tasks and the date they are expected to report on their results.

- Summarize the discussion with a set of final sketches of the agreed upon functionality, layout, or navigation.

- Attempt to obtain agreement from all participants regarding the general direction of the task flow diagram that has been mapped out during the meeting.

- Differences of opinion should be noted. You may find that you'll need to create two or three diagrams that illustrate these competing solutions. Further meetings may be required to resolve the differences.

Summary

The research phase of the design process is perhaps the most indeterminate when it comes to scripting a plan to enact. I have briefly covered: the objective of holding stakeholder interviews, the importance of establishing design tenets, the benefits of doing a competitive analysis, the concept behind running a heuristic evaluation, how to create personas, and the value of card sorting, user surveys, and brainstorming.

Further exploration and study of these and other research methods will definitely be needed before you will feel confident in your decisions. Though just a brief primer, an understanding of the techniques I have briefly described should get you pointed in the right direction.

Now that we have a brief overview of some of the more common UX research techniques, let's review some of the more popular information architecture and visual design techniques.

5

Information Architecture and Visual Design Techniques

In this chapter, we will examine just a few of the many information -architecture-related techniques that have been developed to assist in the filtering and ordering of information. Of the few that I have included, I have really only scratched the surface with my brief explanation of how they work and what they do. I would recommend researching these techniques and methodologies further by finding more examples and discussions about them online or by searching out related UX design reference materials.

Information architecture techniques

Task flow diagrams and wireframes are the primary methods used to architect, design, and document our site or application. The information needed to fill in the details of these deliverables will be captured during the research phase. However, we will still need some help in filtering and organizing the data collected. The techniques shown here are aimed at doing just that. Again, we'll need to familiarize ourselves with these techniques to know when it's appropriate to utilize each one.

Reality mapping

Reality mapping is a technique that helps us understand and document the existing task flow of a website or application. In a way, it's a little bit like card sorting; however, it offers a bit more detail. This exercise can be done alone, but is made much more effective and fun when completed with a group. The process requires a wall, a marker, a stack of different colored sticky notes, and access to the site or application we need to redesign.

The goal of this exercise is to document the construction of a product as we journey through it. In addition to capturing the different steps required to complete our desired tasks, we will also document the different questions, concerns, and ideas that come to us along the way. Our end result will look something like the following diagram:

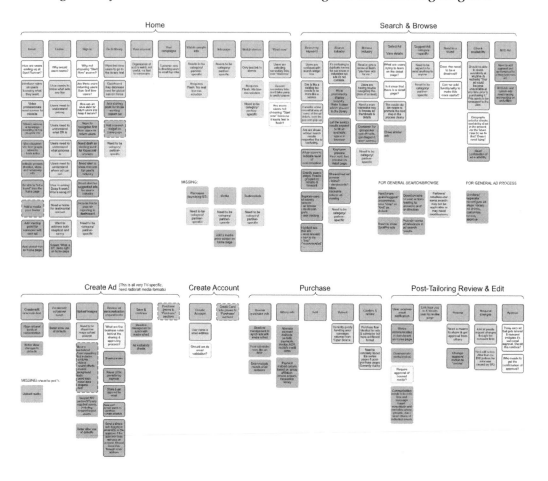

This particular map was generated to help understand a client's complex web application that required redesigning.

As we can see from the preceding example, we started on the home page and created groupings of notes about the experience as we worked our way through the entire product.

We wrote the title of each step in the process on a blue sticky note and placed it on the wall in the order in which it occurred. As we examined each step, we used the other sticky note colors to document our questions (yellow notes), comments and concerns (pink notes), and our new ideas and suggestions (green notes).

After the reality mapping session, we cleaned up our notes by documenting them in our wireframing application of choice.

A detailed view of a single page in the process looked something like the following figure:

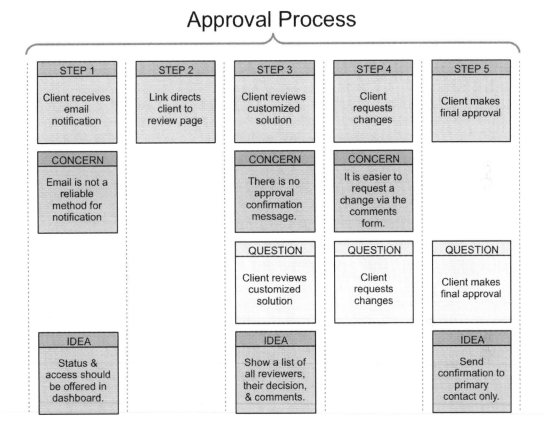

As we can see from this example, the steps in the approval process are documented in blue across the top. Below each step are the associated concerns, questions, and ideas we have for each step.

We can make the most of our reality mapping session by defining the color meanings at the start, and have a means for all to view the site or application being examined during the session. Ensure all participants have a small stack of notes and a pen, and invite them to get out of their seats and add their notes to the chart on the wall at any time.

By the end of the session, we will have not only documented the existing task flow process, but also captured a great deal of valuable information that should help us define how the flow should be reordered and what type of corrections or additions need to be made to the interface.

This technique was created by John Pruitt and Tamara Adlin. More can be learned about this in their book titled *The Persona Lifecycle* (published by *Morgan Kaufmann* in 2006).

Task flow techniques

There are several task flow diagram variations that are worth considering. They all have the same core objective of mapping out the flow of ordered steps in a process, but offer slight differences regarding the granularity of the data they include.

Page-level detail diagrams

This is a diagram that maps out every step of a task that is found on a single screen or page of the product. In the following example, the user is being asked to specify the options required when selecting to add a door to their house and the subsequent decisions it requires:

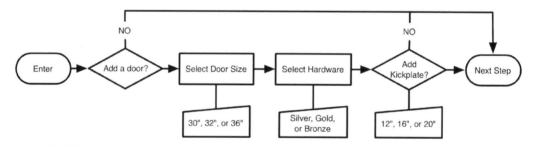

As we can see from this example, the flowchart explains the steps and options that the user has to select from on a single page of an experience. Each decision point in the diagram is represented by a diamond shape, steps by a rectangle, and options to choose from are represented by a manual entry shape.

Site map diagrams

Site maps are fairly straightforward and easy to comprehend. Each page of the site is represented by a rectangle. Arrows show how the user can navigate from one page to another, thus showing an at-a-glance view of the entire site.

Applications can be mapped out the same way, although they usually contain more complex interactions that require more than the standard rectangle shape to explain. This is the most commonly created task flow diagram solution.

 Searching the Internet for "UX task flow diagram" will return many more examples and suggestions for their usage.

The following diagram shows a simple example of a site map:

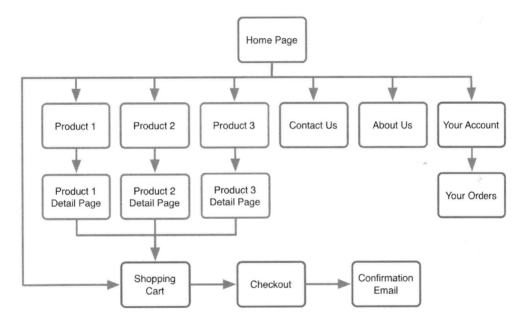

Persona-based task flow diagrams

Mapping out the expected task flow, or the anticipated navigational path each of our personas is likely to follow, can add insight into the overall navigability of our site or application. To create this style of diagram, we start by assigning each persona its own color. We then illustrate their paths through the site map. This technique can help communicate the differences expected for each user type and can help us see how a single screen or page may need to offer multiple messages or solutions to address each unique viewpoint:

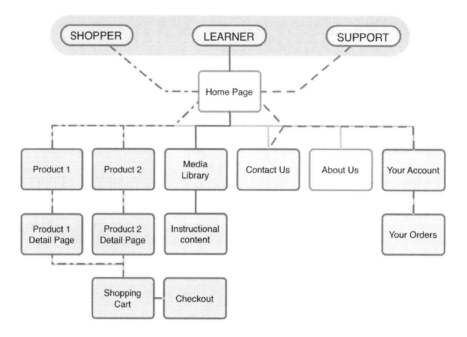

In the preceding example, we show the path of someone shopping, someone looking to gather information, and another user who is seeking answers about a shipment or otherwise needing customer service support. The chart allows us to trace their most likely path. The preceding diagram shown is rather basic, and thus might show how to create this type of diagram, but might not fully illustrate its benefit. This type of diagram can be particularly helpful when we have user profiles that are very different from one another. It can help ensure that each user type gets the messaging and interface elements needed to accomplish their specific set of tasks.

Screenshot interaction maps

This method uses small screenshots, mockups, or wireframes instead of basic shapes to illustrate the task flow. The following diagram is an example utilizing the wireframes from *Chapter 3, Example Project – Mobile Device Application*:

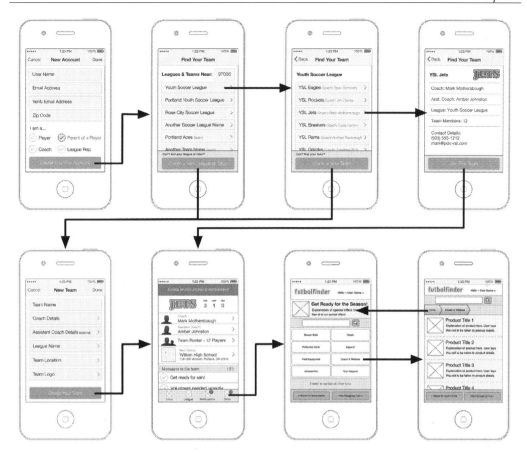

This technique is often used to document the layout of a site or application when working on a redesign. As we might expect, the added detail can help by mapping out a comprehensive set of interactions, while at the same time showing the entire site or application with enough detail that it can be understood at a glance.

Paper prototyping

Paper prototyping is an effective and inexpensive method for testing the effectiveness of our wireframes. This technique is simply the act of printing out our wireframes on paper and letting a test participant walk through them as though they were actually using the finished product. We place the printout of the interface in front of the test participant and ask what they would do to complete a specific task. We then swap out the printouts with the appropriate pages that match their path through the product. If they decide to click on a certain button, we place the page that the button leads to in front of them.

One benefit of this technique is the ability to write down the user's comments directly on the page. We can cross out items they don't like, flag areas of confusion, and so on. It can make the experience much more interactive, and breaks down the barrier usually experienced when testing software on the screen. In such situations, it is common for the test participant to feel like it is an IQ test that they must pass or fail. This can cause them some embarrassment if they don't understand the interface. Having this test take place on paper can help the user feel like they are participating in the construction effort, rather than trying to understand a finished product or having their intelligence tested.

One common drawback of paper prototyping is the difficulty of managing a large number of printouts. It's fairly easy with smaller products, but it can be extremely difficult to manage products with complex interactions. In these situations, we may wish to hold the test directly in the wireframing application itself. Wireframing applications such as Axure, Omnigraffle, and Visio all allow us to apply links to any page element. So, if a button is clicked, it will automatically take the user to the page we connect it to. This doesn't give us the same benefits of taking notes as the paper prototype version does, but it can make for a cleaner and faster test.

Visual design techniques

I've touched very lightly on the visual design aspect. Though very much connected with UX design, it is in reality a unique discipline. There are, however, a couple of techniques that we might consider using or at least need to be aware of.

Mood boards

If you've ever worked with a client and had them attempt to verbally explain the visual style they want for their product, you are likely to know how difficult that can be to understand. I once had a client explain the style they were looking for with the following sentence: "I want it to be like Van Gogh meets Andy Warhol, but you know, like modern and fresh." Clearly this client had a specific idea in their mind's eye, but their attempt to translate that into words did not help explain it to me in the slightest. If anything, I was more confused than edified by their explanation.

For many years, interior and graphic designers have used mood boards, or "inspiration boards", to aid their attempts to quickly capture and communicate the essence or mood of a particular style. The technique involves making a collection or collage of objects that represent the direction we would like our visual design to go in. These objects are usually glued to a poster board or in a large notebook.

The most common objects added are magazine clippings that have a certain shared quality or theme. But it can be anything from a specific color palette, line weight, attitude, facial expression, font, or iconic element. I have also seen things such as buttons, ticket stubs, rope, paint chips, rocks, leaves, and sticks glued to boards. The only limitation I suppose is portability. The following is an example of a mood board:

Inspire mood board used by kind permission of Melanie Augustin

This collection of physical objects, printouts, and clippings will act as our muse when we set out to create the product's visual style and ethos. Involving the client in its creation is a good way to ensure that we are capturing the images they have in their heads. If our client is not entirely certain of the visual direction, the creation of a few boards containing varying styles can really help them make a decision. Furthermore, it seems to help them commit to the selected style, reducing the tendency some clients have of requesting a change in direction midway through the project.

Design scorecard

Similar to the design tenet scorecard mentioned earlier, this is an interface and visual design scorecard. I developed this with Seattle-based designer Michael Kunz in 2004, while working together on a project for Amazon.com. We faced difficulties with certain members of the organization who were causing us a great deal of frustration during the review process. They were very passionate and outspoken. So much so that they were sinking entire design solutions just because they didn't like a particular aspect of it. In normal situations, this is not a significant issue. We simply fix the portion someone doesn't like. That was not working for us in this particular instance. In an attempt to solve this situation, we quantified the different parts of the design into commonly valued visual attributes and placed these attributes on a scorecard. During our review of the mockups, we handed out the scorecards and invited the team members to document their opinions for each category. This allowed our outspoken individual to provide a low rating for the part that offended them and examine the other attributes separately. This individualization of attributes, as well as the normalization of values that occurred when tallying up the other scorecards, helped put the objections into perspective for the rest of the team. We were then able to precisely define the problem element and fix it without throwing out the entire solution.

This is not a technique to use with every design review we hold. It might, however, help us work through some of our more difficult reviews by offering some perspective.

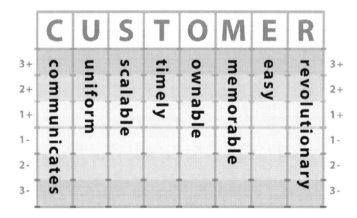

The following is a description of the design attributes found in the preceding chart. Each attribute adds it's first letter to the word "CUSTOMER" to remind us whose point of view this should be scored from:

- **C—Communicates**: This attribute implies that an information hierarchy is established. There is a clear flow of content, and things are messaged clearly and are easily understandable.

- **U—Uniform**: This denotes that there is consistency in the UI, look and feel, and task flow. The design fits in the macro view of the site.

- **S—Scalable**: This means there is graceful adaptation to the growing amounts of information, partners, or uses. The design is easily reproduced on a large scale.

- **T—Timely**: This indicates that the design/experience is in keeping with current industry standards.

- **O—Ownable**: This means the design/experience is unique to our company or client. It stands out in comparison to the competition as being uniquely our own.

- **M—Memorable**: This implies the design is remembered and referred to when not using the site.

- **E—Easy**: This indicates usability and intuition and that the design is easy to navigate and easily understood. Help is available and useful. The navigation and presentation of the features is intuitive to use, offering the user a clearly understood task flow.

- **R—Revolutionary**: This denotes innovations that set the pace for us and for our competition.

Designing in the browser

Designing in the browser is an emerging technique that is a response to the difficulty found when designing interfaces containing complex interactions and responsive design considerations.

Basically put, the mockup stage that normally takes place in applications such as Photoshop is completed directly in HTML and CSS. The result is a prototype of sorts that can be previewed in the browser as it is designed.

The benefits of this melding of design and development are rapidly growing. Traditional static mockups have never been truly "pixel perfect." Due to the limitations of HTML and CSS, there has almost always been some deviation from what was designed in Photoshop when the final product is produced. Furthermore, it is growing increasingly difficult to demonstrate complex interactions and how the page will flex or respond to different screen sizes with static mockups. Creating multiple mockups to illustrate the effects of *fluid* and *responsive* design techniques can require a lot of time and effort. Designing in the browser can make the job much easier.

As we might expect, this requires that we possess some frontend development skills. However, this situation is changing. Applications such as Macaw (`http://macaw.co/`) are being developed to help designers with a more WYSIWYG solution.

This methodology is growing in popularity, but is not a panacea for every project. It can still be easier to explore our initial style in Photoshop or other graphic editing applications. Often a client will want to see examples of several different visual directions before committing to one. It would likely be overkill to generate an HTML version of each. Once our style is established, however, designing in the browser can speed up our design and development process dramatically.

We'll need to give careful consideration as to when this technique is appropriate to employ. It may require the addition of some more technical skills to our bag of tricks, but its advantages are significant.

Summary

Though only a handful of the many techniques related to information architecture and visual design are covered in this chapter, an understanding of these methodologies should help us get started.

Utilizing techniques such as reality mapping, paper prototyping, and the various task flow diagramming techniques illustrated in this chapter will help us organize our content to establish a cohesive and thorough design solution.

Employing methodologies such as mood boards, design scorecards, and designing in the browser can help us work through the subjectivity often found in the visual design phase. They can speed up the design process and help us communicate with our clients more effectively.

Further exploration and study of these and other information architecture and visual design methods will be needed before we feel fully confident using the design process. Though just a brief primer, I have briefly described an understanding of the techniques, which should get us pointed in the right direction.

I hope you have found this introduction to the industry standard design process and explanation of commonly used design techniques beneficial and insightful. There is much more to study and apply, but you should now possess the fundamentals of wireframing and user experience design. I am confident that applying the design principles illustrated in this book will help you avoid the many pitfalls inherent in the software design process.

I wish you success in all that you design.

Index

A

adaptive design 16
agile environment
  designing in 10

B

brainstorming
  about 78
  guidelines 78, 79
breadcrumb navigation model 61
browser
  designing in 91, 92

C

card sorting 77
category pages
  wireframing 38-40
client personas
  developing 48-50
  Eric Enthusiast 49
  Peter Player 49
  Susan Soccermom 48
Coach & Referee category button 65
competitive analysis 72

D

delivery phase
  about 19
  working 19, 20
design attributes
  C-Communicates 90
  E-Easy 91
  M-Memorable 91

  O-Ownable 91
  R-Revolutionary 91
  S-Scalable 91
  T-Timely 91
  U-Uniform 91
design decisions
  usability testing 66
design process
  about 5
  delivery phase 19, 20
  information architecture 10-16
  researching 7-10
  research techniques 8
  stages 6
  visual design 17, 18
design research
  about 7
  agile development methodologies 10
  importance 8, 9
  techniques 8
design scorecard
  about 90
  design attributes 90
  working 90
design tenet scorecard
  about 70
  working 71, 72
development efforts
  reviewing 46

E

e-commerce website
  designing 23
e-commerce website, designing
  development efforts, reviewing 46

Information Architecture 31-45
  research 24-31
End Users Licensing Agreement (EULA) 56

F

Feature Reality Test
  running through 50, 51
flowchart development 11
flowchart shapes
  defining 12-15
fluid design technique 91
focus groups 77

H

heuristic evaluation 75, 76
home page
  initial homepage wireframe 35
  refined homepage wireframe 37, 38
  wireframing 33-35
  wireframing applications 35

I

information architecture
  about 10
  content, wireframing 33
  delivery 45, 46
  flowchart development 11
  flowchart shapes, defining 12-15
  interaction map, creating 51-54
  mockups 45-60
  objective 11
  pages, wireframing 33
  site map, creating 32, 33
  sketches 55-60
  usability testing 17
  wireframe 15, 16
information architecture techniques
  about 81
  paper prototyping 87, 88
  reality mapping 81-84
  task flow techniques 84-87
interaction maps
  creating 51-53
  second version 53, 54

M

Macaw
  URL 91
Minimum Viable Product (MVP) 47, 72
mood boards
  about 88
  using 88, 89

N

navigation options
  about 61
  global navigation 61
  navigation, removing 62
  portal navigation 61

P

personas
  about 73
  creating 73-75
product detail pages
  wireframing 40, 41

R

reality mapping
  about 81
  goal 82
  using 82-84
research techniques
  about 69
  brainstorming 78, 79
  card sorting 77
  competitive analysis 27, 72
  design tenet scorecard 70-72
  features, prioritizing 29-31
  features, weighing 29-31
  focus groups 77
  heuristic evaluation 75, 76
  personas 27, 28, 73
  personas, creating 73-75
  personas, defining 27
  stakeholder interviews 25, 26, 70
  user profiles 73
  user surveys 78
responsive design technique 16, 91

S

shopping cart
  wireframing 42, 43
site map
  creating 32, 33
sketches
  about 55
  deliverables, presenting 66
  Futbol Finder storefront 62-64
  new account, creating 55, 56
  product category, shopping by 65, 66
  team, finding 57, 58
  team homepage 60
  team, joining 58
stakeholder interviews 70
stakeholders
  interviewing 48-50

T

task flow techniques
  about 84
  page-level detail diagrams 84
  persona-based task flow diagrams 86
  screenshot interaction maps 86, 87
  site map diagrams 85

U

usability testing 17
user profiles 73
user surveys 78

V

video library page
  wireframing 43-45
visual design
  about 17
  visual layer, applying 18
visual design techniques
  about 88
  designing in browser 91, 92
  design scorecard 90, 91
  mood boards 88, 89

W

waterfall methodology 10
wireframes
  deliverables, presenting 66
  transitioning to 15, 16
wireframing techniques 17

Thank you for buying
Wireframing Essentials
An introduction to user experience design

About Packt Publishing

Packt, pronounced 'packed', published its first book "*Mastering phpMyAdmin for Effective MySQL Management*" in April 2004 and subsequently continued to specialize in publishing highly focused books on specific technologies and solutions.

Our books and publications share the experiences of your fellow IT professionals in adapting and customizing today's systems, applications, and frameworks. Our solution based books give you the knowledge and power to customize the software and technologies you're using to get the job done. Packt books are more specific and less general than the IT books you have seen in the past. Our unique business model allows us to bring you more focused information, giving you more of what you need to know, and less of what you don't.

Packt is a modern, yet unique publishing company, which focuses on producing quality, cutting-edge books for communities of developers, administrators, and newbies alike. For more information, please visit our website: www.packtpub.com.

Writing for Packt

We welcome all inquiries from people who are interested in authoring. Book proposals should be sent to author@packtpub.com. If your book idea is still at an early stage and you would like to discuss it first before writing a formal book proposal, contact us; one of our commissioning editors will get in touch with you.

We're not just looking for published authors; if you have strong technical skills but no writing experience, our experienced editors can help you develop a writing career, or simply get some additional reward for your expertise.

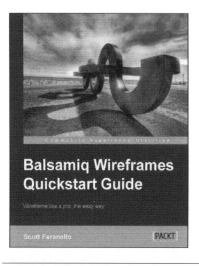

Balsamiq Wireframes Quickstart Guide

ISBN: 978-1-84969-352-3   Paperback: 142 pages

Wireframe like a pro, the easy way

1. A simple yet professional approach to wireframing and prototyping using Balsamiq Mockups

2. Practice essential wireframing skills using real-world examples and challenging exercises

3. Build simple, interactive, clickable, and effective prototypes with Balsamiq

GIMP 2.6 cookbook

ISBN: 978-1-84951-202-2   Paperback: 408 pages

Over 50 recipes to produce amazing graphics with the GIMP

1. Recipes for working with the GIMP, the most powerful open source graphics package in the world

2. Straightforward instructions guide you through the tasks to unleash your true creativity without being hindered by the system

3. Part of Packt's cookbook series — practical and efficient

Please check **www.PacktPub.com** for information on our titles

Getting Started with Lumion 3D

ISBN: 978-1-84969-949-5   Paperback: 134 pages

Create a professional architectural visualization in minutes using Lumion 3D

1. A beginner's guide to architectural visualization

2. Tips and tricks for modeling, texturing, and rendering using Lumion 3D

3. Add a special touch to your images with Photoshop

Axure RP 6 Prototyping Essentials

ISBN: 978-1-84969-164-2   Paperback: 446 pages

Creating highly compelling, interactive prototypes with Axure that will impress and excite decision makers

1. Quickly simulate complex interactions for a wide range of applications without any programming knowledge

2. Acquire timesaving methods for constructing and annotating wireframes, interactive prototypes, and UX specifications

3. A hands-on guide that walks you through the iterative process of UX prototyping with Axure

Please check **www.PacktPub.com** for information on our titles